Better Homes and Gardens.

Dinner in a Bowl

160 recipes for simple, satisfying meals

WILEY

John Wiley & Sons, Inc.

Meredith Corporation

Editor: Jan Miller

Contributing Editor: Lisa Kingsley, Waterbury Publications, Inc.

Recipe Development and Testing: Better Homes and Gardens Test Kitchen

John Wiley & Sons, Inc.

Publisher: Natalie Chapman

Executive Editor: Anne Ficklen

Senior Editor: Linda Ingroia

Production Editor: Abby Saul

Production Director: Diana Cisek

Interior Design and Layout: Tai Blanche

Manufacturing Manager: Tom Hyland

Test Kitchen

Our seal assures you that every recipe in *Dinner in a Bowl* has been tested in the Better Homes and Gardens® Test Kitchen. This means that each recipe is practical and reliable and meets our high standards of taste appeal. We guarantee your satisfaction with this book for as long as you own it.

Published by John Wiley & Sons, Inc., Hoboken, New Jersey

Published simultaneously in Canada

For general information on our other products and services or for technical support, please contact our Customer Care Department within the United States at (800) 762-2974, outside the United States at (317) 572-3993 or fax (317) 572-4002.

Wiley publishes in a variety of print and electronic formats and by print-on-demand. Some material included with standard print versions of this book may not be included in e-books or in print-on-demand. If this book refers to media such as a CD or DVD that is not included in the version you purchased, you may download this material at http://booksupport.wiley.com. For more information about Wiley products, visit www.wiley.com.

Library of Congress Cataloging-in-Publication Data:

Better homes and gardens dinner in a bowl: 160 recipes for simple, satisfying meals
      p. cm.
   Includes index.
   ISBN 978-1-118-03815-4 (pbk.), 978-1-118-11983-9 (ebk.), 978-1-118-11984-6 (ebk.), 978-1-118-11985-3 (ebk.)
   1. Casserole cooking. 2. One-dish meals. 3. Quick and easy cooking. I. Better Homes and Gardens Books (Firm)
   TX693.B497 2012
   641.82'1--dc23

                                        2011029027

Printed in the United States of America

10 9 8 7 6 5 4 3 2 1

CONTENTS

Introduction

From Pad Thai to Beef Stroganoff to Buffalo Chicken Salad, some of the world's best food is served up in a bowl.

There's something uniquely satisfying about a one-bowl meal. The saucy, soupy, creamy dishes that necessitate being eaten out of a bowl are the essence of comfort food. They provide soothing sustenance to smooth out the rough edges of a long day. And when you're in the mood for a different kind of food—something light and healthful—a bowl is the perfect vessel for serving crisp, main-dish green salads and potluck-perfect pasta salads.

Better Homes and Gardens Dinner in a Bowl includes more than 160 recipes for one-dish meals inspired by foods from all over the globe. Chapters include:

The Asian Bowl: Sauced, stir-fried, or swirled into soup, these bowls are inspired by noodle shops and home kitchens from Tokyo to Bangkok to Mumbai.

The European Bowl: From French Cassoulet to Provençal Seafood Stew to oodles of noodles from Italy, these recipes cover the continent.

The American Bowl: Find up-to-date takes on chili, chicken and dumplings, jambalaya, and beef and noodles, along with lots of fresh new ways to fill the dinner bowl.

The Salad Bowl: From the noodle salads of Asia to a French-American take on Salade Niçoise to classic American Chicken Caesar Salad, these main-dish salads take their inspiration from everywhere.

Each chapter contains classic recipes perfect for puttering in the kitchen on a leisurely Saturday afternoon, as well as dozens of weeknight meals that go together in 30 minutes or less. These quick recipes feature fun flavor twists and creative uses of ingredients and cooking methods so you can get dinner on the table as fast as possible.

Each chapter also features a Make-It-Mine master recipe that can be customized according to what you're craving—or what you have on hand.

A set of at-a-glance icons helps you choose just the right recipe for your needs. Look for these designations throughout the book:

30 MINUTES

KID-FRIENDLY

HEALTHFUL

SHARE WITH FRIENDS (suitable for entertaining)

All of the recipes in *Dinner in a Bowl* have been tested in the Better Homes and Gardens Test Kitchen, so you know they work and taste great. No matter what you choose to make, you'll be filling your dinner bowl with delicious, nutritious, soul-satisfying food.

The Asian bowl

Chinese egg noodles

Wonton wrappers

Cellophane

Superthin bahn pho

Ramen

Thin bahn pho

Medium bahn pho

Somen

Thick bahn pho

Buckwheat vermicelli

Udon

Soba

Asian Noodles

1. Chinese egg noodles: Made from eggs and wheat, these noodles are pale yellow in color. They come in several shapes and sizes and are often sold in bundles.

2. Wonton wrappers: Paper-thin squares of dough made from flour, water, eggs, and salt. To make dumplings for soup, wonton skins are filled with seasoned minced meat or seafood and cooked in broth.

3. Cellophane noodles: Made from mung bean starch, these chewy but ethereal noodles turn translucent when cooked. They are also called glass noodles or bean threads.

4. Superthin rice noodles: Made from rice flour, these noodles are very popular in Southeast Asia. Rice noodles come in several different sizes (see #5, #6, and #7). Thinner noodles are best used in soups, salads, and spring rolls. Every country has a different name for essentially the same noodle. The most common variety in the United States is Vietnamese *bahn pho*. Almost all rice noodles need to be soaked in hot water until they are soft and translucent before using. Read the package instructions to be sure.

5. Thin rice noodles: Like the superthin rice noodles, these are best used in soups, salads, and spring rolls. Look for them in the Asian section of your supermarket or at an Asian market.

6. Medium rice noodles: These midsize strands are the most versatile of the rice noodles. They can be used in soups, salads, and stir-fries.

7. Thick rice stick noodles: Chewy and substantial, these noodles are best used in stir-fries.

8. Ramen: The name *ramen* is from the brothy Japanese dish in which these delicate wheat noodles are used. However, they are actually called *chukamen* noodles and are the type most commonly used in ramen dishes. Because the name *ramen* has become so common, you will find this type of noodle labeled both ways.

9. Buckwheat vermicelli: Korean noodles made from buckwheat flour and rice or potato starch. They are very similar to Japanese soba (see #12).

10. Somen: Very thin, delicate Japanese wheat noodles almost always served cold.

11. Udon: Slippery and substantial, these thick Japanese wheat noodles are best used in soups and stews.

12. Soba: Japanese noodles made with a blend of buckwheat and wheat flours. The buckwheat flour gives the noodles a dark brownish gray color and a distinctively nutty, earthy flavor.

Bibimbap

PREP: 45 MINUTES   **COOK:** 30 MINUTES

2   **cups water**

¼   **teaspoon salt**

1   **cup long grain rice**

3   **tablespoons chili paste (Korean Gochujang is traditional)**

2   **tablespoons rice vinegar**

1   **tablespoon honey**

1   **teaspoon toasted sesame oil**

2   **6-ounce beef rib-eye steaks, ½ inch thick**

1½   **cups very thinly sliced seedless cucumber**

¼   **cup finely chopped scallions (2)**

2   **cups mung bean sprouts**

2   **tablespoons sesame oil (not toasted)**

1   **teaspoon grated fresh ginger**

1   **pound fresh spinach leaves**

3   **tablespoons toasted sesame seeds**

2   **cloves garlic, minced**

1½   **cups packaged fresh julienned or shredded carrots**

6   **ounces shiitake mushrooms, stemmed and sliced**

2   **eggs**

1   **cup coarsely shredded daikon**

1 In a medium saucepan bring the water and ¼ teaspoon salt to boiling over medium-high heat. Stir in rice; cover. Reduce heat to medium low; simmer for 12 minutes. Remove from heat and let stand.

2 In a small bowl whisk together chili paste, vinegar, honey, and toasted sesame oil. If necessary, add a little water to make mixture of drizzling consistency. Brush steaks with 1 tablespoon of the chili paste mixture; set steaks aside.

3 In a small bowl combine the cucumber, scallions, and 1 teaspoon of the chili paste mixture; season lightly with additional salt and set aside.

4 Transfer hot cooked rice to a large platter. In a large pot of boiling water cook and stir bean sprouts for 1 minute. With a slotted spoon, transfer sprouts to a medium bowl, shaking off excess water. While still warm, add 2 teaspoons of the untoasted sesame oil and the ginger; toss to coat. Transfer to rice-lined platter.

5 In same pot of water cook and stir spinach about 10 seconds or just until cooked. Drain in a colander. When cool enough to handle squeeze out excess water and coarsely chop. Transfer to a medium bowl; add sesame seeds and lightly season with additional salt. Toss to coat and transfer to platter next to bean sprouts.

6 In a medium skillet heat 1 teaspoon of the remaining untoasted sesame oil over medium-high heat. Add garlic; cook and stir for 30 seconds. Add carrots; cook and stir about 2 minutes or until crisp-tender. Transfer to platter next to sprouts.

7 In same skillet heat 2 teaspoons of the remaining untoasted sesame oil over medium-high heat. Add mushrooms; cook and stir for 3 to 4 minutes or until just tender. Stir in 1 teaspoon of the chili paste mixture. Transfer to platter next to carrots.

8 In a large skillet heat 2 teaspoons of the remaining untoasted sesame oil over medium-high heat. Add steaks; reduce heat to medium. Cook about 7 minutes, turning once, or until desired doneness. Remove to a cutting board and cover with foil. Add cucumber mixture to skillet; cook and stir just until heated through. Add to platter.

9 In same skillet add remaining sesame oil and heat over medium heat. Add eggs; cook 1 to 2 minutes or until yolks are just set.

10 Arrange daikon on platter. Thinly slice the beef and arrange over vegetables. Top with eggs and drizzle with 1 tablespoon chili paste mixture. To serve at the dinner table, toss all together, breaking up eggs. Serve with remaining chili paste mixture. **Makes 4 to 6 servings**

Nutrition facts per serving: 651 cal., 32 g total fat (10 g sat. fat), 164 mg chol., 619 mg sodium, 64 g carb., 8 g dietary fiber, 12 g sugar, 29 g protein.

Bowl Bit The name of this colorful and eye-catching Korean dish (pronounced BEE-beem-bop) literally means "mixed meal." It is generally a bowl of cooked rice topped with vegetables, meat, chili paste, and an egg. The ingredients are placed next to each other instead of layered so that the bright colors of the vegetables and the egg complement each other. In some variations, the dish is served in a very hot stone bowl. The raw egg is cooked against the side of the bowl and the rice at the bottom gets brown and crispy from sizzling in sesame oil at the bottom of the pot. Right before the dish is eaten, the ingredients are all tossed together.

Asian Beef and Noodle Bowl

START TO FINISH: 30 MINUTES

4 cups water

2 3-ounce packages ramen noodles

2 teaspoons chili oil or vegetable oil*

12 ounces beef flank steak or beef top round steak, cut into bite-size strips

1 teaspoon grated fresh ginger

2 cloves garlic, minced

1 cup beef broth

1 tablespoon soy sauce

2 cups torn fresh spinach

1 cup shredded carrots (2 medium)

¼ cup snipped fresh mint or cilantro

¼ cup chopped peanuts (optional)

1 In a large saucepan bring the water to boiling. If desired, break up noodles; drop noodles into the boiling water. (Do not use the flavor packets.) Return to boiling; boil for 2 to 3 minutes or just until noodles are tender but firm, stirring occasionally. Drain noodles.

2 In a wok or large skillet heat oil over medium-high heat. Add beef, ginger, and garlic; cook and stir for 2 to 3 minutes or to desired doneness. Push beef from center of the wok. Add beef broth and soy sauce. Bring to boiling; reduce heat. Add meat to broth mixture; cook and stir for 1 to 2 minutes more or until heated through.

3 Add noodles, spinach, carrots, and mint to meat mixture; toss to combine. Ladle mixture into soup bowls. If desired, sprinkle with peanuts. **Makes 4 servings**

Nutrition facts per serving: 211 cal., 10 g total fat (3 g sat. fat), 47 mg chol., 690 mg sodium, 11 g carb, 2 g dietary fiber, 20 g protein.

*Note: *If using vegetable oil, stir ⅛ to ¼ teaspoon cayenne pepper into the oil.*

Chinese Hot Pot

PREP: 1 HOUR 10 MINUTES **COOK:** 5 MINUTES

8 ounces fresh or frozen, peeled, and deveined shrimp

8 ounces fresh or frozen sole, cut into 2-inch pieces

1 recipe Dipping Sauce

8 ounces boneless beef top loin steak

3 cups shredded napa cabbage

1 cup sliced shiitake mushrooms

1 cup bean sprouts, trimmed

1 cup thinly bias-sliced carrots (2 medium)

1 8-ounce can sliced bamboo shoots, drained

8 cups water

1 teaspoon salt

2 tablespoons sliced scallion (1)

1 inch fresh ginger, peeled and thinly sliced

4 ounces dried wide rice stick noodles

1 Thaw shrimp and fish, if frozen. Meanwhile, prepare Dipping Sauce.

2 If desired, brown steak on both sides in a lightly oiled large skillet over medium-high heat. Transfer beef to a cutting board. Thinly slice beef into bite-size strips. Arrange beef on a platter. Rinse shrimp and fish; pat dry with paper towels. Add shrimp and fish to platter; set aside.

3 Arrange cabbage, mushrooms, bean sprouts, carrots, and bamboo shoots on a separate platter; set aside.

4 In a large saucepan bring the water and salt to boiling. Pour boiling water into a firepot, electric wok, or electric skillet. Light burner under pot or preheat wok or skillet to medium heat.

5 To serve, give each person a bowl and a small wire strainer, chopsticks, or a slotted spoon. Dip meat, fish, and shrimp into simmering water until done. Allow 30 to 60 seconds for beef or until it reaches desired doneness, 1 to 2 minutes for fish or until it flakes easily with a fork, and 1 or 2 minutes for shrimp or until opaque. Remove from water and place in bowls. Add cabbage, mushrooms, bean sprouts, carrots, and bamboo shoots to pot; cook for 1 to 2 minutes or until crisp-tender. Remove from water and add to bowls. When all meat, fish, shrimp, and vegetable mixture are cooked, add scallion, ginger, and noodles to broth. Cook about 3 minutes or until noodles are tender. Remove and discard ginger pieces. Pour broth and noodles over meat and vegetables in bowls. Stir Dipping Sauce into each bowl to taste. **Makes 6 to 8 servings**

Nutrition facts per serving: 270 cal., 5 g total fat (1 g sat. fat), 93 mg chol., 1,293 mg sodium, 29 g carb., 3 g dietary fiber, 4 g sugar, 26 g protein.

Dipping Sauce: In a small bowl stir together ½ cup reduced-sodium soy sauce; ¼ cup snipped fresh cilantro; ¼ cup sliced scallions (2); 1 tablespoon toasted sesame oil; 1 small fresh jalapeño chile pepper, seeded and finely chopped* (optional); 2 teaspoons sugar; 2 teaspoons rice vinegar; 2 teaspoons grated fresh ginger; and 2 cloves garlic, minced. Cover and allow to stand for 1 hour before serving. Makes about ¾ cup.

***Note:** Because chile peppers contain volatile oils that can burn your skin and eyes, avoid direct contact with them as much as possible. When working with chile peppers, wear plastic or rubber gloves. If your bare hands do touch the peppers, wash your hands and nails well with soap and warm water.*

Bowl Bit Sometimes called "Mongolian hot pot," this dish of meat, vegetables, and noodles cooked at the table in boiling water or broth has a history that goes back more than 1,000 years. There is some speculation that a very rudimentary version of it was created by Mongol warriors who cooked food in their helmets. The dipping sauce that now accompanies this versatile dish would have been a welcome addition!

Spicy Beef and Broccoli Noodle Bowl

START TO FINISH: 20 MINUTES

- 1 pound boneless beef sirloin steak, cut into thin strips
- 1 tablespoon vegetable oil
- 2 14-ounce cans reduced-sodium beef broth
- ⅓ cup bottled peanut sauce
- 3 ounces dried medium egg noodles (1½ cups)
- 2 cups broccoli florets
- ¼ cup bias-sliced scallions (optional)

1 In a Dutch oven, brown beef strips in hot oil over medium-high heat. Add beef broth and peanut sauce; bring to boiling.

2 Stir in noodles; reduce heat. Simmer, uncovered, for 4 minutes, stirring occasionally to separate noodles. Add broccoli; return to boiling. Reduce heat. Simmer, uncovered, for 3 to 4 minutes more or just until noodles are tender, stirring occasionally.

3 Divide beef and noodle mixture among bowls. Sprinkle with scallions. **Makes 4 servings**

Nutrition facts per serving: 316 cal., 12 g total fat (3 g sat. fat), 60 mg chol., 762 mg sodium, 18 g carb., 2 g dietary fiber, 5 g sugar, 31 g protein.

Tangerine Beef with Asparagus and Glass Noodles

PREP: 40 MINUTES   **MARINATE:** 2 TO 8 HOURS   **COOK:** 8 MINUTES

- 1 **pound flank steak**
- ¼ **cup soy sauce**
- ¼ **cup rice wine (mirin)**
- 2 **tablespoons finely shredded tangerine zest**
- 1 **tablespoon sesame oil**
- 2 **teaspoons cornstarch**
- 2 **cloves garlic, minced**
- 1 **teaspoon crushed red pepper**
- ¾ **cup thinly sliced scallions, white part only**
- 2 **tablespoons minced garlic**
- 1 **tablespoon grated fresh ginger**
- ½ **cup reduced-sodium chicken broth**
- ¼ **cup tangerine juice**
- 2 **tablespoons ponzu sauce**
- 2 **tablespoons soy sauce**
- 4 **ounces bean threads (glass noodles)**
- ¼ **cup peanut oil**
- ½ **bunch asparagus, bias-sliced into 3-inch pieces**
- ½ **cup chopped fresh cilantro**
- ⅓ **cup finely chopped dried apricots (optional)**

1 If desired, partially freeze beef for easier slicing. Trim fat from meat. Thinly slice meat across the grain into ¼-inch-thick slices. Place beef in a large resealable plastic bag set in a shallow dish. For marinade, combine ¼ cup soy sauce, rice wine, 1 tablespoon of the tangerine zest, the sesame oil, cornstarch, 2 cloves garlic, and crushed red pepper. Pour marinade over beef in bag; seal bag. Marinate in the refrigerator for 2 to 8 hours. Drain meat, discarding marinade.

2 In small bowl combine scallions, 2 tablespoons garlic, ginger, and remaining tangerine zest. Set aside.

3 In a another small bowl combine chicken broth, tangerine juice, ponzu sauce, and 2 tablespoons soy sauce. Set aside.

4 Place bean threads in a large bowl. Add enough hot tap water to cover. Let stand about 5 minutes or until soft and pliable; drain well. Using kitchen shears, cut into 4-inch lengths.

5 In a large wok or extra-large skillet heat oil over high heat. Reduce heat to medium. Add scallion mixture; cook and stir over medium heat about 30 seconds. Add beef strips; cook and stir about 2 minutes or until no longer pink. Add asparagus; cook and stir for 1 minute. Stir in broth mixture; bring to simmering. Stir in reserved noodles; cook and stir until heated through.

6 Divide mixture evenly among serving bowls. Garnish with cilantro and, if desired, dried apricots. Serve immediately. **Makes 6 servings**

Nutrition facts per serving: 336 cal., 17 g total fat (4 g sat. fat), 26 mg chol., 1,313 mg sodium, 28 g carb., 1 g dietary fiber, 5 g sugar, 19 g protein.

Kitchen Tip Bean thread noodles, also called cellophane or glass noodles, are made from mung bean starch. When cooked, they turn opaque and delightfully chewy. Be careful not to overcook them—they quickly lose their toothsome quality.

Pork and Yellow Rice with Vegetables

START TO FINISH: 30 MINUTES

- 2 tablespoons olive oil or vegetable oil
- 1 pound lean boneless pork, cut into 1-inch pieces
- ¾ teaspoon cumin seeds, crushed
- 1 medium onion, halved and sliced
- 2 cloves garlic, minced
- 1 cup peeled baby carrots
- 1½ cups cauliflower florets
- 1 14-ounce can reduced-sodium chicken broth
- 1 cup water
- ½ teaspoon ground turmeric
- 1⅓ cups long grain rice
- ¼ cup sliced scallions (2)

1 In a large skillet heat oil over medium-high heat. Add pork and cumin seeds; cook and stir for 2 minutes. Add onion and garlic; cook and stir for 2 minutes more. Drain off fat.

2 Cut any large carrots in half lengthwise. Add carrots, cauliflower, broth, the water, and turmeric to skillet. Stir in rice. Bring to boiling; reduce heat. Simmer, covered, about 15 minutes or until rice is tender. Stir mixture gently. Sprinkle with scallions. **Makes 5 or 6 servings**

Nutrition facts per serving: 403 cal., 12 g total fat (3 g sat. fat), 50 mg chol., 387 mg sodium, 46 g carb., 2 g dietary fiber, 2 g sugar, 25 g protein.

Shanghai Pork Lo Mein

START TO FINISH: 25 MINUTES

- 8 ounces dried somen noodles, fine egg noodles, or angel hair pasta
- 2 teaspoons olive oil or vegetable oil
- 8 ounces pork tenderloin, halved lengthwise and sliced ¼ inch thick
- 2 cups sliced bok choy
- 1 cup reduced-sodium chicken broth
- ¼ cup orange juice
- 3 tablespoons reduced-sodium soy sauce
- 2 teaspoons toasted sesame oil
- ¼ to ½ teaspoon crushed red pepper
- 1 11-ounce can mandarin orange sections, drained

1 Cook noodles or pasta according to package directions; drain.

2 Meanwhile, in a large skillet heat oil over medium-high heat. (If necessary, add more oil during cooking.) Add pork to skillet; cook and stir for 3 minutes. Add bok choy; cook and stir about 2 minutes more or until pork is no longer pink and bok choy is crisp-tender.

3 Combine broth, orange juice, soy sauce, sesame oil, and crushed red pepper. Add to skillet; bring to boiling. Add noodles to skillet mixture; toss. Cook for 1 minute, stirring occasionally. Serve in bowls with orange sections. **Makes 4 servings**

Nutrition facts per serving: 349 cal., 7 g total fat (1 g sat. fat), 36 mg chol., 1,667 mg sodium, 50 g carb., 3 g dietary fiber, 6 g sugar, 20 g protein.

The Asian Bowl | 23

Singapore Noodles

PREP: 15 MINUTES   **COOK:** 25 MINUTES

6   ounces medium rice noodles, broken

2   tablespoons canola oil

1   tablespoon curry powder

½   teaspoon ground coriander

½   cup chicken broth

1½   tablespoons reduced-sodium soy sauce

2   teaspoons Asian chili sauce

2   tablespoons oyster sauce

2   teaspoons grated fresh ginger

2   cloves garlic, finely chopped

6   ounces lean boneless pork, cut into bite-size strips

6   ounces medium shrimp, peeled and deveined

1   medium red sweet pepper, cut into thin strips

4   ounces shiitake mushrooms, stemmed and sliced

3   cups shredded napa cabbage

4   scallions, trimmed and cut into 1-inch pieces

1   cup fresh or thawed frozen peas

2   eggs, lightly beaten

     Asian chili sauce (optional)

1 Prepare noodles according to package directions.

2 Meanwhile, in a medium saucepan heat 2 teaspoons of the oil over medium heat. Add curry powder and coriander; cook for 1 minute. Add broth, soy sauce, and 2 teaspoons Asian chili sauce. Bring to a simmer. Add oyster sauce; remove from heat.

3 In a large skillet or wok heat 2 teaspoons of the remaining oil over medium-high heat. Add ginger and garlic; cook for 30 seconds. Add pork; cook and stir for 2 minutes. Add shrimp; cook and stir for 2 to 3 minutes more or until shrimp are opaque. Transfer pork and shrimp to saucepan with chili sauce mixture.

4 Add the remaining oil to skillet. Add sweet pepper and mushrooms; cook and stir for 4 minutes. Add cabbage, scallions, and peas; cook and stir for 3 to 4 minutes or until vegetables are crisp-tender.

5 Push mixture to the sides of skillet. Add eggs to center of skillet and cook, without stirring, for 1 to 2 minutes or until eggs begin to set. Stir eggs and vegetables together. Drain noodles. Add with pork mixture to skillet; cook and stir until heated through. Serve immediately with additional Asian chili sauce, if desired. **Makes 4 servings**

Nutrition facts per serving: 441 cal., 13 g total fat (2 g sat. fat), 197 mg chol., 799 mg sodium, 53 g carb., 5 g dietary fiber, 5 g sugar, 27 g protein.

Thai Curry Cellophane Noodles

PREP: 20 MINUTES   **COOK:** 10 MINUTES

1 **3.75-ounce package dried cellophane (bean thread) noodles**

1 **tablespoon cornstarch**

1 **cup light unsweetened coconut milk**

1 **tablespoon canola oil**

¼ **cup chopped onion**

1 **cup chopped red sweet pepper (1 medium)**

¼ **cup chopped scallions (2)**

2 **teaspoons minced fresh ginger**

1 **clove garlic, minced**

1 **teaspoon curry powder**

¼ **teaspoon kosher salt**

1 **pound pork tenderloin, cut into bite-size pieces**

1 **tablespoon lime juice**

1 **tablespoon chopped fresh parsley or cilantro**

1 Place noodles in a large bowl. Add enough hot tap water to cover. Let stand for 10 minutes or until pliable but not soft; drain well. Cut noodles into smaller strands; Set aside; keep warm.

2 In a small bowl stir together cornstarch and coconut milk; set aside.

3 In a wok or large skillet heat oil over medium heat. Add onion; cook and stir for 2 minutes. Add sweet pepper, scallions, ginger, garlic, curry powder, and salt; cook and stir for 2 minutes more. Add pork; cook and stir for 3 to 4 minutes or until pork is brown and no longer pink.

4 Push pork and vegetables from center of wok. Stir lime juice into coconut mixture. Add to center of wok; cook and stir until thickened and bubbly. Cook and stir pork, vegetable, and sauce mixture for 1 minute more. Serve over noodles. Sprinkle with parsley. **Makes 4 servings**

Nutrition facts per serving: 311 cal., 10 g total fat (4 g sat. fat), 73 mg chol., 200 mg sodium, 29 g carb., 1 g dietary fiber, 1 g sugar, 24 g protein.

Thai Pork and Vegetable Curry

START TO FINISH: 30 MINUTES

1¹/₃ cups jasmine rice

12 ounces pork tenderloin or lean boneless pork

Salt and ground black pepper

2 tablespoons vegetable oil

8 ounces green beans,* bias-sliced into 1½-inch pieces (2 cups)

1 red sweet pepper, cut into thin bite-size strips

2 scallions, bias-sliced into ¼-inch pieces

1 14-ounce can unsweetened coconut milk

4 teaspoons bottled curry paste

1 teaspoon sugar

¹/₈ teaspoon crushed red pepper

Hot cooked rice

1 lime, cut into wedges

1 Cook rice according to package directions. Keep warm.

2 Meanwhile, thinly slice pork into bite-size strips. Sprinkle with salt and pepper. In a large nonstick skillet heat 1 tablespoon of the oil over medium-high heat. Add pork; cook and stir about 4 minutes or until no pink remains. Remove from skillet.

3 Add the remaining oil to skillet. Add green beans; cook and stir for 3 minutes. Add sweet pepper and scallions; cook and stir about 2 minutes more or until vegetables are crisp-tender. Remove from skillet. Add coconut milk, curry paste, sugar, and crushed red pepper to skillet. Bring mixture to boiling; reduce heat. Simmer, uncovered, about 2 minutes or until mixture is slightly thickened. Stir in pork and vegetables; heat through. Serve over hot cooked rice with lime wedges. **Makes 4 servings**

Nutrition facts per serving: 490 cal., 16 g total fat (5 g sat. fat), 47 mg chol., 593 mg sodium, 63 g carb., 3 g dietary fiber, 4 g sugar, 23 g protein.

*Note: *A 9-ounce package of frozen cut green beans, thawed, can be substituted for the fresh beans. Add them to the skillet along with the sweet pepper and scallions; cook as directed.*

Lamb and Garbanzo Bean Curry

START TO FINISH: 45 MINUTES

12 ounces boneless lamb shoulder roast

2 tablespoons all-purpose flour

¼ teaspoon salt

1 cup chopped onion (1 large)

1 clove garlic, minced

2 tablespoons vegetable oil

1 tablespoon curry powder

1½ cups reduced-sodium chicken broth

1 15-ounce can garbanzo beans, rinsed and drained

1 14.5-ounce can tomatoes, undrained and cut up

4 cups coarsely chopped spinach

1 Trim fat from meat. Cut meat into 1-inch pieces. In a plastic bag combine flour and salt. Add meat pieces, a few at a time, shaking to coat.

2 In a large saucepan or Dutch oven cook onion and garlic in hot oil over medium heat about 4 minutes or until onion is tender. Add meat; cook and stir for 4 to 5 minutes or until meat is brown. Stir in curry powder; cook and stir for 30 seconds more.

3 Add broth to saucepan. Bring to boiling; reduce heat. Simmer, covered, for 20 minutes, stirring occasionally. Stir in garbanzo beans and tomatoes. Bring to boiling; reduce heat. Simmer, covered, for 10 minutes more or until meat is tender, stirring occasionally. Remove from heat. Add spinach, stirring just until wilted. Serve immediately. **Makes 4 or 5 servings**

Nutrition facts per serving: 413 cal., 23 g total fat (7 g sat. fat), 58 mg chol., 954 mg sodium, 28 g carb., 10 g dietary fiber, 5 g sugar, 24 g protein.

Chicken Pad Thai

PREP: 35 MINUTES   COOK: 12 MINUTES

- 8 ounces dried rice noodles (Vietnamese banh pho or Thai sen-mee)
- ¼ cup salted peanuts, finely chopped
- ½ teaspoon grated lime zest
- 3 tablespoons fish sauce
- 2 tablespoons fresh lime juice
- 2 tablespoons packed brown sugar
- 4½ teaspoons rice vinegar
- 1 tablespoon Asian chili sauce with garlic
- 1 pound boneless, skinless chicken breasts, cut into bite-size strips
- 1 tablespoon finely chopped garlic
- 3 tablespoons vegetable oil
- 1 egg, lightly beaten
- 1 cup bean sprouts
- ⅓ cup sliced scallions (3)
- 2 tablespoons snipped fresh cilantro

1 Place noodles in a large bowl. Add enough hot tap water to cover. Let stand for 10 to 15 minutes or until pliable but not soft; drain well.

2 Meanwhile, for peanut topping, combine peanuts and lime zest; set aside. In a small bowl combine fish sauce, lime juice, brown sugar, vinegar, and chili sauce; stir until smooth. Set aside.

3 In a very large nonstick skillet cook chicken and garlic in 1 tablespoon hot oil over medium-high heat about 6 minutes or until chicken is no longer pink. Transfer chicken to a bowl. Add egg to hot skillet; cook for 30 seconds. Turn egg with spatula and cook for 30 to 60 seconds more or just until set. Remove and chop egg.

4 In the same skillet heat remaining oil over medium-high heat for 30 seconds. Add sprouts and drained noodles; stir-fry for 2 minutes. Add fish sauce mixture and chicken; cook for 1 to 2 minutes or until heated through. Divide mixture among bowls. Sprinkle each serving with egg and peanut topping. Garnish with scallions and cilantro. **Makes 4 servings**

Nutrition facts per serving: 565 cal., 19 g total fat (3 g sat. fat), 119 mg chol., 945 mg sodium, 63 g carb., 3 g dietary fiber, 9 g sugar, 34 g protein.

Chicken Tikka Masala

PREP: 40 MINUTES   MARINATE: 4 HOURS   BROIL: 12 MINUTES   COOK: 18 MINUTES   OVEN: BROIL

1 cup plain yogurt

2 tablespoons lemon juice

1 tablespoon grated fresh ginger

2 teaspoons ground cumin

1 teaspoon ground coriander

½ teaspoon salt

½ teaspoon coarsely ground black pepper

½ teaspoon cayenne pepper

¼ teaspoon ground cardamom

¼ teaspoon ground cinnamon

12 skinless, boneless chicken thighs

2 tablespoons butter

1 fresh jalapeño chile pepper, seeded and finely chopped*

2 cloves garlic, minced

1 15-ounce can crushed tomatoes, undrained

1 tablespoon garam masala

2 teaspoons ground coriander

1½ teaspoons ground cumin

½ teaspoon salt

1 cup whipping cream

4 cups hot cooked basmati rice**

½ cup coarsely chopped fresh cilantro

1 For marinade, in a nonmetal bowl combine yogurt, lemon juice, ginger, 2 teaspoons cumin, 1 teaspoon coriander, ½ teaspoon salt, black pepper, cayenne pepper, cardamom, and cinnamon. Add chicken thighs; turn to coat with marinade. Cover and marinate in refrigerator at least 4 hours, turning chicken occasionally.

2 Preheat broiler. Drain chicken, discarding marinade. Place chicken in a lightly greased broiler pan. Broil 6 inches from heat about 6 minutes or until light brown. Turn chicken and broil for 6 minutes more or until no longer pink. Keep warm.

3 In a large skillet melt butter over medium heat. Add chile pepper and garlic; cook for 1 to 2 minutes or until garlic is tender. Stir in tomatoes, garam masala, 2 teaspoons coriander, 1½ teaspoons cumin, and ½ teaspoon salt. Bring to boiling; reduce heat. Simmer, covered, for 10 minutes. Stir in cream. Return to boiling; reduce heat. Simmer, uncovered, for 5 to 6 minutes or until mixture is slightly thickened. Add chicken; turn to coat with sauce.

4 To serve, divide rice among bowls. Place chicken thighs on rice and spoon sauce over top. Sprinkle with cilantro. Serve immediately. **Makes 6 servings**

Nutrition facts per serving: 544 cal., 25 g total fat (13 g sat. fat), 182 mg chol., 678 mg sodium, 43 g carb., 2 g dietary fiber, 5 g sugar, 35 g protein.

Note: *Because hot chile peppers contain volatile oils that can burn your skin and eyes, avoid direct contact with chiles as much as possible. When working with chile peppers, wear plastic or rubber gloves. If your bare hands do touch the chile peppers, wash your hands well with soap and water.*

****Note:*** *Cook 1⅓ cups basmati rice in 2⅔ cups water or other liquid.*

Kitchen Tip Garam masala is an Indian spice blend made up of some combination of black and white pepper, cloves, mace, cumin, cinnamon, cardamom, nutmeg, star anise, and coriander seeds. Though the name means "hot mixture," it does not have the heat of dried chiles. The word *garam*, or "hot," really just refers to the intensity of the spices. If you can't find it at your regular supermarket, check in an Indian market or online.

Basil Chicken in Coconut-Curry Sauce

1 **tablespoon curry powder**

½ **teaspoon salt**

¼ **teaspoon ground black pepper**

1 **pound skinless, boneless chicken breast halves, cut into 1-inch pieces**

1 **cup chopped red onion (1 large)**

5 **cloves garlic, minced**

2 **fresh jalapeño chile peppers, seeded and finely chopped***

1 **tablespoon olive oil**

1 **13.5 or 14-ounce can unsweetened coconut milk**

2 **teaspoons cornstarch**

3 **tablespoons snipped fresh basil**

1 **tablespoon finely chopped fresh ginger**

3 **cups hot cooked rice**

   Fresh basil leaves (optional)

1 In a medium bowl stir together curry powder, salt, and pepper. Add chicken; toss to coat. Cover and let stand at room temperature for 30 minutes. (Or cover and chill for 1 to 2 hours.)

2 In a large nonstick wok or skillet cook and stir onion, garlic, and chile peppers in hot oil over medium-high heat for 2 minutes. Remove onion mixture from wok. Add half of the chicken to wok; cook and stir for 2 to 3 minutes or until chicken is no longer pink. Remove chicken from the wok; add to onion mixture. (If necessary, add additional oil.) Repeat with remaining chicken. Remove from wok.

3 In a small bowl whisk together the coconut milk and cornstarch. Carefully add to wok; cook and stir until bubbly. Return the chicken and onion mixture to wok. Stir in snipped basil and ginger; cook and stir about 2 minutes more or until heated through. Serve over rice. If desired, garnish with basil leaves. **Makes 4 servings**

Nutrition facts per serving: 522 cal., 26 g total fat (19 g sat. fat), 66 mg chol., 370 mg sodium, 42 g carb., 2 g dietary fiber, 32 g protein.

*Note: *Because chile peppers contain volatile oils that can burn your skin and eyes, avoid direct contact with them as much as possible. When working with chile peppers, wear plastic or rubber gloves. If your bare hands do touch the chile peppers, wash your hands well with soap and water.*

Kitchen Tip If you can find Thai basil, try it in this dish. Thai basil has a more pronounced licorice flavor than the more common sweet basil. Either type will work just fine, though.

Chicken Lo Mein

PREP: 35 MINUTES   **STAND:** 20 MINUTES   **COOK:** 16 MINUTES

- **12 ounces skinless, boneless chicken breast halves**
- **6 tablespoons reduced-sodium soy sauce**
- **1 tablespoon rice vinegar**
- **4 teaspoons sugar**
- **10 ounces dried Chinese egg noodles or linguine**
- **⅓ cup reduced-sodium chicken broth**
- **2 teaspoons cornstarch**
- **1 tablespoon vegetable oil**
- **1 tablespoon sesame oil**
- **4 cloves garlic, minced**
- **1 medium carrot, cut into matchsticks**
- **1 cup chopped bok choy**
- **4 scallions, cut into 2-inch matchsticks**
- **Tamari sauce (optional)**

1 Cut chicken into bite-size strips. In a medium bowl combine 2 tablespoons of the soy sauce, the vinegar, and 2 teaspoons of the sugar. Add chicken; toss to coat. Let stand at room temperature for 20 minutes. (Or cover and chill for 1 hour.)

2 Cook noodles according to package directions until tender; drain. Rinse with cold water; drain well. Set aside. For sauce, in a small bowl stir together broth, cornstarch, remaining soy sauce, and remaining sugar. Set aside.

3 In a wok or large nonstick skillet heat vegetable and sesame oils over medium-high heat. Add garlic; cook and stir for 30 seconds. Add carrot; cook and stir for 2 minutes. Add bok choy and scallions; cook and stir for 2 minutes more. Remove vegetables from wok.

4 Drain chicken, discarding marinade. Add chicken to wok (if necessary, add more oil); cook and stir for 3 to 4 minutes or until no longer pink. Push chicken from center of wok. Stir sauce; add to center of wok; cook and stir until thickened and bubbly. Add cooked noodles and vegetables. Using two spatulas or wooden spoons, lightly toss mixture until combined and heated through. Transfer to a serving platter. Serve immediately, with tamari sauce, if desired. **Makes 6 servings**

Nutrition facts per serving: 326 cal., 7 g total fat (1 g sat. fat), 73 mg chol., 615 mg sodium, 42 g carb., 2 g dietary fiber, 7 g sugar, 22 g protein.

Bowl Bits The word *mein* or *mian* is the Chinese word for "noodles." *Lo mein* means "tossed noodles." Lo mein is always made with Chinese egg noodles made from wheat flour. The soft noodles soak up the yummy sauce.

Cranberry Chicken Biryani
(Mughlai Chicken-Rice Pilaf)

PREP: 40 MINUTES   **MARINATE:** 2 HOURS   **COOK:** 30 MINUTES   **STAND:** 5 MINUTES

1 **pound skinless, boneless chicken breast halves**

1 **6-ounce carton plain yogurt**

1 **tablespoon grated fresh ginger**

4 **cloves garlic, minced**

2 **teaspoons garam masala**

3 **large onions, peeled and thinly sliced**

⅓ **cup butter**

⅔ **cup raw cashews, coarsely chopped**

5 **cups reduced-sodium chicken broth**

2 **cups basmati rice**

1 **tablespoon butter**

1 **teaspoon ground cinnamon**

1 **teaspoon ground cumin**

½ **teaspoon salt**

¼ **teaspoon ground cloves**

½ **cup dried cranberries**

½ **teaspoon cayenne pepper**

1 **cup hot whole milk**

2 **tablespoons chopped fresh mint**

¼ **cup chopped fresh cilantro**

1 Cut chicken into bite-size pieces. In a medium nonmetal bowl combine yogurt, ginger, garlic, and garam masala. Mix well. Add chicken pieces; toss to combine. Cover and marinate in refrigerator for at least 2 hours.

2 In a 5- to 6-quart Dutch oven cook onions in ⅓ cup hot butter, stirring often, about 15 minutes or until onions are golden and caramelized. Using tongs, remove onions from Dutch oven; set aside. Add cashews to Dutch oven; cook for 2 to 3 minutes or until lightly brown and toasted. Using a slotted spoon, remove cashews from Dutch oven; drain on paper towel–lined plate.

3 In a large saucepan combine 4 cups of the chicken broth, the basmati rice, and 1 tablespoon butter. Bring to boiling; reduce heat. Simmer, covered, about 20 minutes or until broth is absorbed and rice is tender. Remove from heat.

4 Drain chicken, discarding marinade. Add chicken to Dutch oven; cook over medium heat for 5 minutes, stirring occasionally. Stir in cinnamon, cumin, salt, and cloves; cook and stir for 1 minute. Add remaining chicken broth; cook and stir for 4 to 5 minutes more or until chicken is tender and no longer pink.

5 Add cranberries, caramelized onions, and cooked rice to chicken mixture in Dutch oven. Mix gently. Combine cayenne pepper and milk. Pour milk mixture over chicken-rice mixture. Cover and let stand for 5 minutes. Remove lid and mix well.

6 To serve, divide chicken mixture among serving bowls. Top with mint, cilantro and reserved cashews. Serve immediately. **Makes 6 to 8 servings**

Nutrition facts per serving: 635 cal., 24 g total fat (11 g sat. fat), 82 mg chol., 850 mg sodium, 76 g carb., 4 g dietary fiber, 16 g sugar, 32 g protein.

Bowl Bit The Mughal people—of Turkish-Persian origins—came to India in the sixteenth century, bringing their cuisine with them. Many of these aromatic dishes featured rice, spices, nuts, raisins, cream, and milk. This contemporary take on biryani calls for the tart twist of cranberries in place of the more traditional golden raisins.

Soba Noodles with Spring Vegetables

START TO FINISH: 25 MINUTES

2   14.5-ounce cans vegetable or chicken broth

2   tablespoons finely chopped fresh ginger

2   tablespoons reduced-sodium soy sauce

1   cup thinly sliced carrots (2 medium)

8   ounces dried soba (buckwheat) noodles or whole wheat spaghetti, broken

2   cups cubed cooked chicken or turkey

2   cups shredded bok choy

1   cup halved peapods

⅔   cup sliced radishes or chopped daikon

1   teaspoon toasted sesame oil

    Scallion strips

1 In a Dutch oven combine broth, ginger, and soy sauce. Bring to boiling; reduce heat. Simmer, covered, for 5 minutes.

2 Add carrots; simmer for 3 minutes. Stir in noodles. (If using whole wheat spaghetti, stir in pasta and cook for 6 minutes before adding carrots.) Bring to boiling; reduce heat. Simmer, uncovered, about 4 minutes or until noodles and carrots are tender. Stir in chicken, bok choy, peapods, radishes, and sesame oil; heat through. Sprinkle each serving with scallion strips. **Makes 4 servings**

Nutrition facts per serving: 276 cal., 8 g total fat (2 g sat. fat), 39 mg chol., 1,092 mg sodium, 37 g carb., 3 g dietary fiber, 22 g protein.

Green Curry Chicken

START TO FINISH: 30 MINUTES

8 ounces dried rice vermicelli noodles or vermicelli

12 ounces skinless, boneless chicken breast halves, cut into bite-size strips

1 tablespoon vegetable oil

1 14-ounce can unsweetened coconut milk

2 tablespoons soy sauce

1 to 2 teaspoons green curry paste

2 cups cauliflower florets

1 medium red sweet pepper, cut into thin strips

½ cup coarsely shredded carrot (1 medium)

1 Cook vermicelli according to package directions; drain and keep warm.

2 Meanwhile, in a large skillet cook chicken in hot oil over medium heat for 3 to 4 minutes or until no longer pink; remove from skillet. Add coconut milk, soy sauce, and curry paste to skillet. Bring to boiling; reduce heat. Gently boil, uncovered, for 5 minutes. Add cauliflower; simmer, uncovered, for 5 minutes. Add sweet pepper, carrot, and chicken. Return to boiling; reduce heat. Simmer, uncovered, about 3 minutes more or until vegetables are crisp-tender. Divide noodles among bowls; top with chicken mixture. **Makes 4 servings**

Nutrition facts per serving: 538 cal., 26 g total fat (20 g sat. fat), 49 mg chol., 633 mg sodium, 56 g carb., 4 g dietary fiber, 15 g sugar, 24 g protein.

Lemongrass Chicken over Noodles

START TO FINISH: 50 MINUTES

2 tablespoons sugar

3 tablespoons water

⅓ cup chicken broth

3 tablespoons fish sauce or oyster sauce

1 teaspoon cornstarch

2 tablespoons vegetable oil

2 tablespoons finely chopped fresh lemongrass, or 1 teaspoon finely shredded lemon zest

3 cloves garlic, minced

1 large onion, halved lengthwise and thinly sliced

1 medium carrot, thinly bias-sliced

2 cups broccoli florets

1 medium red or green sweet pepper, cut into 1-inch squares

2 fresh red Fresbi chile peppers, seeded and cut into thin strips*

12 ounces skinless, boneless chicken breasts or thighs, cut into bite-size strips

3 cups hot cooked Chinese egg noodles, vermicelli, capellini, fettuccine, or linguine

Snipped fresh cilantro (optional)

1 For sauce, in a small saucepan heat sugar over medium-high heat until sugar begins to melt, shaking saucepan occasionally to heat sugar evenly. Reduce heat to low; cook until sugar is melted and light brown, about 3 minutes more. Stir as necessary after sugar begins to melt. Carefully add the water, stirring until sugar is dissolved. Remove from heat. Stir together broth, fish sauce, and cornstarch; stir into sugar mixture. Set aside.

2 In a wok or large skillet heat oil over medium-high heat (if necessary, add more oil during cooking). Stir-fry lemongrass and garlic in hot oil for 15 seconds. Add onion and carrot; stir-fry for 2 minutes. Add broccoli; stir-fry for 2 minutes. Add sweet pepper and chile pepper; stir-fry about 2 minutes more or until vegetables are crisp-tender. Remove vegetables from wok.

3 Add chicken to wok; stir-fry about 4 minutes or until no longer pink. Push chicken from center of wok. Stir sauce; add to center of wok. Cook and stir until thickened and bubbly. Return cooked vegetables to wok; cook and stir about 1 minute or until heated through. Serve chicken and vegetable mixture over noodles. If desired, sprinkle with cilantro. **Makes 4 servings**

Nutrition facts per serving: 405 cal., 10 g total fat (2 g sat. fat), 89 mg chol., 1,201 mg sodium, 50 g carb., 5 g dietary fiber, 29 g protein.

*Note: *Because chile peppers contain volatile oils that can burn your skin and eyes, avoid direct contact with them as much as possible. When working with chile peppers, wear plastic or rubber gloves. If your bare hands do touch the peppers, wash your hands and nails well with soap and warm water.*

Chicken and Cauliflower Curry

START TO FINISH: 40 MINUTES

2 tablespoons vegetable oil

2 pounds skinless, boneless chicken, cut into 1-inch pieces

½ cup chopped onion (1 medium)

4 teaspoons curry powder

1 tablespoon chopped fresh ginger

¼ teaspoon cayenne pepper

1 large head cauliflower, cut into florets (4 cups)

1 medium green sweet pepper, cut into 1-inch pieces

1 14-ounce can chicken broth

2 tablespoons cornstarch

1 15- to 16-ounce can garbanzo beans (chickpeas), rinsed and drained

1 14.5-ounce can diced tomatoes, undrained

½ teaspoon salt

Snipped fresh cilantro

Hot cooked rice (optional)

1 In a nonstick 4-quart Dutch oven heat 1 tablespoon of the oil over medium-high heat. Add half of the chicken pieces; cook for 5 minutes or until cooked through, stirring occasionally. Remove to a plate and set aside. Repeat with remaining chicken.

2 Add remaining oil to Dutch oven. Add onion; cook and stir over medium-high heat for 2 minutes. Add curry powder, ginger, and cayenne pepper; cook and stir for 1 minute. Stir in cauliflower and sweet pepper.

3 In a small bowl stir together ¼ cup of the chicken broth and cornstarch. Stir remaining broth, garbanzo beans, tomatoes, and salt into cauliflower mixture. Bring to boiling; reduce heat. Cover and simmer for 10 minutes, stirring occasionally.

4 Stir in cornstarch mixture; cook and stir until thickened and bubbly. Cook and stir for 2 minutes more. Add chicken; heat through. Top each serving with cilantro. If desired, serve with rice. **Makes 8 servings**

Nutrition facts per serving: 356 cal., 16 g total fat (5 g sat. fat), 41 mg chol., 648 mg sodium, 31 g carb., 7 g dietary fiber, 5 g sugar, 21 g protein.

Thai Chicken Big Bowl

PREP: 30 MINUTES   **COOK:** 6 MINUTES

2 tablespoons vegetable oil

1 pound skinless, boneless chicken breast halves, cut into 1-inch cubes

4 teaspoons bottled minced garlic, or 8 cloves garlic, minced

4 teaspoons minced fresh ginger

1 tablespoon red curry paste, or ¼ teaspoon cayenne pepper

1 teaspoon ground cumin

4 cups water

1 14-ounce can unsweetened coconut milk

2 cups shredded carrots (4 medium)

2 cups small broccoli florets

1 medium red sweet pepper, cut into bite-size strips

2 3-ounce packages chicken-flavor ramen noodles, coarsely broken

2 cups snow peas halved crosswise

2 tablespoons soy sauce

4 teaspoons lime juice

1 cup sliced fresh basil

⅓ cup snipped fresh cilantro

1 In a 4-quart Dutch oven heat 1 tablespoon of the oil over medium-high heat. Add chicken; cook and stir for 3 to 4 minutes or until no longer pink. Remove chicken from Dutch oven.

2 Add remaining oil to Dutch oven. Add garlic, ginger, curry paste, and cumin; cook and stir for 30 seconds. Stir in the water, coconut milk, carrot, broccoli, sweet pepper, and noodles (set seasoning packets aside). Bring to boiling; reduce heat. Simmer, covered, for 3 minutes. Stir in cooked chicken, peapods, seasoning packets, soy sauce, and lime juice. Stir in basil and cilantro. Serve in soup bowls. **Makes 6 servings**

Nutrition facts per serving: 454 cal., 25 g total fat (12 g sat. fat), 44 mg chol., 1,087 mg sodium, 33 g carb., 4 g dietary fiber, 4 g sugar, 26 g protein.

Thai Rice Noodles

PREP: 20 MINUTES   COOK: 8 MINUTES

12 ounces fresh rice noodles
    (rice ribbon noodles)

3 tablespoons vegetable oil

12 ounces skinless, boneless chicken
    breast halves, cut into bite-size
    pieces

1 tablespoon minced fresh ginger

2 cloves garlic, minced

2 cups broccoli florets

2 carrots, cut into thin bite-size pieces
    (1 cup)

1 small onion, cut into thin wedges
    (⅓ cup)

¼ cup oyster sauce

1 tablespoon packed brown sugar

1 Cut rice noodles into strips 1 inch wide and 3 to 4 inches long. In a large skillet heat 2 tablespoons of the oil over medium-high heat for 1 minute. Carefully add noodles; cook and stir for 3 to 4 minutes or until edges of noodles just begin to turn golden. Remove noodles from skillet.

2 Add remaining oil, chicken, ginger, and garlic to skillet; cook and stir for 2 to 3 minutes or until chicken is no longer pink. Stir in broccoli, carrots, and onion; cook and stir for 2 to 3 minutes more or until vegetables are crisp-tender. Stir in oyster sauce, brown sugar, and noodles; heat through. **Makes 4 servings**

Nutrition facts per serving: 341 cal., 12 g total fat (2 g sat. fat), 49 mg chol., 507 mg sodium, 37 g carb., 2 g dietary fiber, 22 g protein.

Thai Curried Noodle Bowl

PREP: 10 MINUTES   **COOK:** 20 MINUTES

- 1 12- to 14-ounce package dried wide rice stick noodles
- 1 tablespoon vegetable oil
- ¾ cup coarsely chopped carrots
- 1 cup sliced shiitake mushrooms, stems removed, or 1 cup sliced white mushrooms
- ¾ cup coarsely chopped red sweet pepper (1 medium)
- 2 scallions, bias-sliced into ¼-inch pieces
- 1 14-ounce can regular or light unsweetened coconut milk
- 3 to 4 teaspoons red curry paste
- 1½ teaspoons sugar
- 2 cups chopped or shredded cooked chicken (about 10 ounces)
- 1 tablespoon lime juice
- ¼ cup chopped dry-roasted peanuts
- 2 tablespoons snipped fresh cilantro

1 In a 4-quart pot cook noodles in lightly salted boiling water for 5 minutes; drain. Return noodles to pot; keep warm.

2 Meanwhile, in a large skillet heat oil over medium-high heat. Add carrots; stir-fry for 3 minutes. Add mushrooms, sweet pepper, and scallions; stir-fry for 2 minutes more. Add coconut milk, curry paste, and sugar. Reduce heat to medium; stir until combined. Add chicken, lime juice, and noodles; heat through. Remove from heat. Add peanuts and cilantro; toss gently to mix.

3 Transfer noodle mixture to a warm serving bowl. Serve immediately. **Makes 4 servings**

Nutrition facts per serving: 776 cal., 35 g total fat (21 g sat. fat), 62 mg chol., 411 mg sodium, 88 g carb., 5 g dietary fiber, 4 g sugar, 29 g protein.

Tom Ka Gai
(Spicy Thai Chicken-Coconut Soup)

PREP: 30 MINUTES **COOK:** 25 MINUTES

2 tablespoons grated fresh ginger

1 teaspoon crushed red pepper

2 tablespoons peanut oil

6 cups reduced-sodium chicken broth

½ cup jasmine rice

3 cups coarsely shredded cooked chicken

1 cup unsweetened coconut milk

1 cup thinly sliced white mushrooms

1 medium red sweet pepper, cut into strips

½ cup chopped onion (1 medium)

¼ cup nam pla (Thai fish sauce)

2 tablespoons chopped fresh cilantro

1 stalk fresh lemongrass, white part only, cut into 1-inch pieces and bruised with the back of a knife

5 fresh kaffir lime leaves, torn in several places toward the spines of the leaves

2 to 3 tablespoons lime juice

Sliced scallions (optional)

Fresh cilantro sprigs (optional)

Lime wedges (optional)

1 In a large saucepan combine ginger, crushed red pepper, and peanut oil; cook and stir over medium heat for 2 minutes. Add broth; bring mixture to boiling. Stir in rice; reduce heat. Simmer, covered, for 15 to 20 minutes or until rice is soft.

2 Add chicken, coconut milk, mushrooms, sweet pepper, onion, fish sauce, chopped cilantro, lemongrass, and lime leaves. Bring to boiling; reduce heat. Simmer, uncovered, for 5 minutes. Using a slotted spoon, remove lemongrass from soup. Stir in lime juice. If desired, garnish with scallions, cilantro, and lime wedges. **Makes 6 servings**

Nutrition facts per serving: 357 cal., 19 g total fat (11 g sat. fat), 62 mg chol., 1,566 mg sodium, 20 g carb., 2 g dietary fiber, 5 g sugar, 26 g protein.

Bowl Bit The key to the fabulousness of Thai food is its perfect balance of spicy, salty, sweet, and sour flavors. This heavenly soup is the epitome of that perfect balance. The sweet comes from coconut milk, the sour from lime, the salty from fish sauce, and the spicy from crushed red pepper.

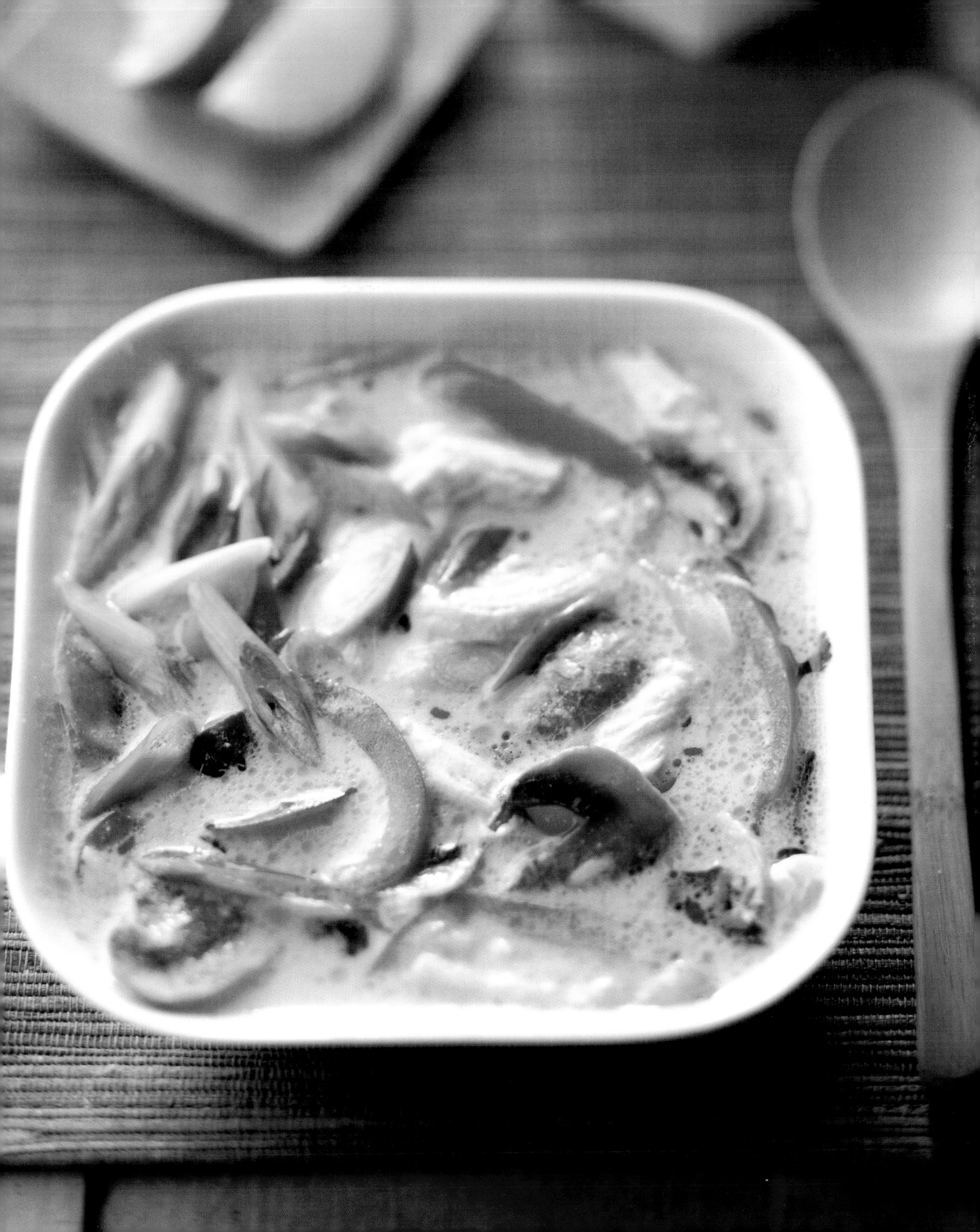

Oyako Donburi (Parent-Child Bowl)

START TO FINISH: 40 MINUTES

1 teaspoon toasted sesame oil

4 eggs

2 tablespoons water

12 ounces skinless, boneless chicken breast halves

1½ cups reduced-sodium chicken broth

1 cup stemmed and sliced shiitake mushrooms

1 8-ounce can bamboo shoots, drained

1 large carrot, cut into julienne strips

½ cup sliced scallions (4)

½ cup frozen green peas

⅓ cup reduced-sodium soy sauce

¼ cup sake

2 tablespoons sugar

1 recipe Sticky Rice

1 In a large skillet heat sesame oil over medium heat. In a small bowl whisk together eggs and the water until combined. Add egg mixture to hot skillet; cook until set, lifting edges so egg mixture flows underneath. Remove skillet from heat. Cover and let stand for 2 minutes. Flip egg mixture out onto cutting board; set aside.

2 Cut chicken into thin bite-size strips (about 1⅔ cups). In same large skillet cook chicken and chicken broth for 3 to 4 minutes or until chicken is no longer pink. Add mushrooms, bamboo shoots, carrot, ¼ cup of the scallions, the peas, soy sauce, sake, and sugar. Return mixture to boiling; reduce heat. Simmer, covered, about 5 minutes or until vegetables are tender.

3 To serve, spoon chicken mixture over hot Sticky Rice in large individual bowls. Garnish with remaining scallions. Divide omelet into 4 wedges. Add a wedge to each bowl. **Makes 4 servings**

Nutrition facts per serving: 409 cal., 8 g total fat (2 g sat. fat), 1295 mg sodium, 49 g carb., 2 g dietary fiber, 31 g protein.

Sticky Rice: Place 1 cup short grain rice in a bowl with cold water. Rub rice with your hands, draining off water and adding fresh water until water is clear. Place rice and 1¾ cups fresh water in a heavy medium saucepan and soak for 45 minutes to 1 hour. Bring rice to boiling over medium-high heat. Reduce heat to medium low; cook, covered, for 10 minutes or until tender. Remove from heat and let stand for 10 minutes.

Bowl Bit In Japanese, *oya* means "parent" and *ko* means "child." *Donburi* means "large bowl." In sum, the fanciful name for this chicken-and-omelet dish is a humorous play on the age-old question of which came first, the chicken or the egg. Individually the chicken and beaten eggs are poached in a broth seasoned with sugar and salty soy sauce and served on sticky rice.

Pacific Rim Shrimp and Snow Peas

START TO FINISH: 25 MINUTES

12 ounces fresh or frozen peeled and deveined medium shrimp

1 tablespoon olive oil or vegetable oil

8 ounces snow peas (2 cups), tips and strings removed

3 cloves garlic, minced

1 teaspoon grated fresh ginger

¼ teaspoon cayenne pepper

¾ cup unsweetened coconut milk

½ teaspoon salt

¼ teaspoon finely shredded lime zest

Hot cooked rice

Lime slices (optional)

1 Thaw shrimp, if frozen. Rinse shrimp; pat dry with paper towels. Set aside.

2 In a large skillet heat oil over medium-high heat. Add snow peas; cook and stir for 2 to 3 minutes or until crisp-tender. Remove snow peas from skillet.

3 Add shrimp, garlic, ginger, and cayenne pepper to skillet; cook and stir about 2 minutes or until shrimp are opaque. Carefully stir in coconut milk, salt, and lime zest; heat until bubbly. Return snow peas to skillet; heat through. Serve over cooked rice. If desired, garnish with lime slices. **Makes 4 servings**

Nutrition facts per serving: 333 cal., 14 g total fat (9 g sat. fat), 129 mg chol., 425 mg sodium, 29 g carb., 2 g dietary fiber, 2 g sugar, 22 g protein.

Curried Coconut Shrimp on Rice Stick Noodles

START TO FINISH: 30 MINUTES

- 6 to 7 ounces dried thin rice stick noodles (vermicelli) or thin spaghetti
- 1 14-ounce can chicken broth
- 2 medium carrots, cut into julienne strips (about 1 cup)
- 2 scallions, bias-sliced into 1¼-inch pieces (¼ cup)
- 2 tablespoons minced fresh ginger
- 2 teaspoons curry powder
- ¼ teaspoon crushed red pepper
- 12 ounces peeled and deveined small fresh or frozen shrimp
- 1 14-ounce can unsweetened coconut milk
- 2 tablespoons coarsely snipped fresh cilantro, basil, or flat-leaf parsley
- 2 tablespoons toasted shaved coconut

1 Cook noodles according to package directions in a large amount of boiling salted water till tender; drain. Rinse with cold water; drain well. Divide noodles among soup bowls. Set aside.

2 In a medium saucepan bring broth to boiling. Add carrots, scallions, ginger, curry powder, and crushed red pepper. Return to boiling; reduce heat. Simmer, uncovered, for 3 minutes, stirring occasionally.

3 Add shrimp. Simmer, uncovered, for 1 to 3 minutes or until shrimp are opaque. Add coconut milk; heat through (do not boil). Ladle into bowls over noodles. Top each serving with cilantro and coconut. Serve immediately. **Makes 4 servings**

Nutrition facts per serving: 479 cal., 22 g total fat (18 g sat. fat), 129 mg chol., 667 mg sodium, 46 g carb., 2 g dietary fiber, 22 g protein.

Green Curry Shrimp

PREP: 15 MINUTES   **COOK:** 20 MINUTES

1½ **pounds large shrimp**

3 **cups water**

1 **cup jasmine rice**

2 **tablespoon vegetable oil**

2 **cloves garlic, minced**

2 **tablespoons green curry paste**

1 **14-ounce can unsweetened coconut milk**

1 **cup chicken broth**

1 **tablespoon fish sauce**

1 **tablespoon sugar**

¼ **teaspoon salt**

8 **ounces haricots verts (thin green beans) or regular green beans, halved lengthwise**

1 **large red sweet pepper, seeded and thinly sliced**

1 **cup shredded carrots (2 medium)**

Lime wedges and/or fresh basil leaves (optional)

1 Peel and devein shrimp. Rinse shrimp; pat dry with paper towels. Set aside.

2 In a large saucepan bring water to boiling. Add rice. Return to boiling; reduce heat. Simmer, covered, about 20 minutes or until tender.

3 Meanwhile, in a large skillet heat oil over medium-high heat. Add garlic; cook for 30 seconds. Add curry paste; cook for 30 seconds more. Whisk in coconut milk, broth, fish sauce, sugar, and salt. Bring to boiling; reduce heat. Simmer, uncovered, about 5 minutes or until slightly thickened, stirring occasionally.

4 Add green beans, sweet pepper, and carrots. Return to boiling. Cook and stir about 5 minutes or until vegetables are just crisp-tender. Add shrimp; cook and stir for 2 to 3 minutes more or until shrimp are opaque and vegetables are just tender.

5 Serve curry mixture over rice. If desired, serve with lime wedges and/or basil leaves. **Makes 6 servings**

Nutrition facts per serving : 484 cal., 24 g total fat (16 g sat. fat), 172 mg chol., 866 mg sodium, 40 g carb., 4 g dietary fiber, 7 g sugar, 28 g protein.

Kitchen Tip Jasmine rice is sometimes called Thai fragrant rice, for its slightly floral aroma and delicate nutty flavor. You can use regular long grain rice if you don't have jasmine rice, but the flavor won't be quite the same.

Sui Gow (Shrimp and Chive Dumpling Bowl)

START TO FINISH: 45 MINUTES

6 ounces fresh or frozen medium shrimp

¼ cup finely chopped and stemmed shiitake mushrooms

3 tablespoons snipped fresh chives

3 whole canned water chestnuts, finely chopped (4 teaspoons)

2 teaspoons cornstarch

1 teaspoon grated fresh ginger

½ teaspoon salt

16 wonton wrappers

1 tablespoon canola oil

⅛ teaspoon crushed red pepper

2 cups sliced and stemmed shiitake mushrooms

5 cups reduced-sodium chicken broth

1 tablespoon reduced-sodium soy sauce

1 tablespoon plum sauce

1 teaspoon rice vinegar

6 baby bok choy, quartered lengthwise (about 1¼ pounds), or 3 cups sliced bok choy

1 Thaw shrimp, if frozen. Peel, devein, and coarsely chop shrimp. Line a baking sheet with parchment paper. In a medium bowl combine shrimp, ¼ cup chopped mushrooms, chives, water chestnuts, cornstarch, ginger, and salt. Place a wrapper in one hand. Spoon about 2 teaspoons of the shrimp mixture into the center of the wrap. Lightly moisten wrap around filling with water. With other hand bring up edges of wrap around filling; press and twist lightly to seal. Place on prepared baking sheet. Repeat with remaining wraps and filling. Cover with plastic wrap; set aside.

2 In a Dutch oven heat oil and crushed red pepper over medium-high heat. Add 2 cups sliced shiitake mushrooms; cook and stir for 2 minutes. Add broth, soy sauce, plum sauce, and vinegar; bring to a simmer. Add bok choy; cook for 4 to 5 minutes or until bok choy is just tender. Reduce heat to low; keep warm.

3 Meanwhile, bring a large pot of lightly salted water to a simmer over medium-high heat. Add wontons; cook about 5 minutes, stirring gently, or until wontons look translucent. Remove with a slotted spoon.

4 Ladle broth, mushrooms, and bok choy into large bowls and top with wontons. **Makes 4 to 6 servings**

Nutrition facts per serving: 269 cal., 5 g total fat (1 g sat. fat), 68 mg chol., 1,492 mg sodium, 39 g carb., 4 g dietary fiber, 3 g sugar, 19 g protein.

Bowl Bit This warming dumpling bowl hails from northern China. Although you can find *sui gow* wrappers at some Asian markets, this simplified version calls for wonton wrappers, which—though thinner than *sui gow* wrappers—are much easier to find.

Soba Noodles in Broth

START TO FINISH: 20 MINUTES

12 ounces fresh or frozen shrimp

8 ounces dried soba (buckwheat noodles) or vermicelli, broken in half

1 14-ounce can reduced-sodium chicken broth

¼ cup sweet rice wine (mirin)

¼ cup reduced-sodium soy sauce

2 teaspoons sugar

½ teaspoon instant dashi granules (dried tuna-and-seaweed-flavor soup stock)

2 scallions, bias-sliced

1 Thaw shrimp, if frozen. Peel and devein shrimp, leaving tails intact, if desired. Rinse shrimp; pat dry with paper towels. Set aside.

2 In a large saucepan cook noodles or vermicelli in a large amount of boiling water about 4 minutes or until tender; drain.

3 Meanwhile, in a medium saucepan combine broth, mirin, soy sauce, sugar, and dashi granules. Bring to boiling; reduce heat. Add shrimp; simmer about 2 minutes or until shrimp are opaque.

4 Divide noodles among serving bowls. Pour shrimp and broth over noodles. Sprinkle with scallions. Serve immediately. **Makes 4 servings**

Nutrition facts per serving: 333 cal., 2 g total fat (0 g sat. fat), 130 mg chol., 1,606 mg sodium, 54 g carb., 3 g dietary fiber, 6 g sugar, 28 g protein.

Kitchen Tip Dashi granules are widely available at Asian markets, as are Japanese soba noodles. Thin, soft, soba are made with buckwheat flour, which gives them their distinct, slightly sweet, nutty flavor and pale purple-gray hue.

Palak Paneer
(Indian Spinach with Paneer Cheese)

PREP: 40 MINUTES   **COOK:** 32 MINUTES

- 3 tablespoons butter
- 1 cup chopped onion (1 large)
- 1 teaspoon cumin seeds
- 1 teaspoon Asian chili sauce
- 1 teaspoon grated fresh ginger
- 2 cloves garlic, minced
- 1 teaspoon garam masala
- ½ teaspoon salt
- 1 cup chopped tomatoes (2 medium)
- 1 bay leaf
- 1 10-ounce package fresh baby spinach, chopped
- 1 cup vegetable oil
- 8 ounces paneer cheese, cut into ¾-inch cubes
- ¼ cup whipping cream

Kitchen Tip Paneer is a fresh, unaged cheese similar to pot cheese that is pressed until it has a firm texture similar to that of firm tofu. You can find it at most Indian markets. If you can't find it, substitute Mexican queso fresco or Greek halloumi.

1 In an extra-large skillet melt butter over medium heat. Add onion and cumin seeds; cook and stir for 4 to 5 minutes or until onion is soft and cumin seeds are toasted. Stir in Asian chili sauce, ginger, garlic, garam masala, and salt. Add tomatoes and bay leaf. Bring mixture to boiling; reduce heat. Simmer, covered, for 10 minutes. Gradually add spinach, stirring after each addition just until wilted. Remove from heat.

2 Meanwhile, in another large skillet heat oil over medium-high heat. Add cheese cubes; cook and turn cheese for 2 to 3 minutes, or until light brown on all sides. Using a slotted spoon, transfer cheese from skillet to a paper towel–lined plate.

3 Add whipping cream to spinach mixture; cook and stir over medium heat for 4 to 5 minutes, or until thickened. Stir in reserved cheese. Serve immediately. **Makes 4 servings**

Nutrition facts per serving: 378 cal., 33 g total fat (13 g sat. fat), 62 mg chol., 520 mg sodium, 13 g carb., 3 g dietary fiber, 3 g sugar, 10 g protein.

Broccoli with Ginger Tofu

START TO FINISH: 25 MINUTES

⅓ cup reduced-sodium chicken broth

3 tablespoons reduced-sodium
   soy sauce

1 tablespoon dry sherry or
   reduced-sodium chicken broth

1 tablespoon grated fresh ginger

2 teaspoons cornstarch

4 cloves garlic, minced

1 tablespoon olive oil or vegetable oil

4 cups broccoli florets

1 medium red sweet pepper, cut into
   thin bite-size strips

8 ounces firm or extra-firm tub-style
   tofu, drained and cut into ½-inch
   cubes

   Hot cooked rice

1 For sauce, combine broth, soy sauce, sherry, ginger, and cornstarch. Set aside.

2 In a large skillet cook garlic in hot oil over medium-high heat for 30 seconds. Add broccoli and sweet pepper; cook and stir for 4 to 5 minutes or until vegetables are crisp-tender.

3 Push vegetables from center of skillet. Stir sauce; add to center of skillet. Cook and stir until thickened and bubbly. Add tofu; cook, stirring gently, for 1 to 2 minutes or until heated through. Stir in vegetables. Serve over rice. **Makes 4 servings**

Nutrition facts per serving: 246 cal., 7 g total fat (1 g sat. fat), 0 mg chol., 508 mg sodium, 34 g carb., 4 g dietary fiber, 2 g sugar, 12 g protein.

Kitchen Tip In any stir-fry dish, be sure to use the firmest tofu you can find. Anything less than "firm" will fall apart when it's cooked.

Indian Lentils and Spinach

PREP: 15 MINUTES   **COOK:** 34 MINUTES

1 cup chopped red sweet pepper (1 medium)

½ cup chopped onion (1 medium)

2 cloves garlic, minced

½ teaspoon curry powder

2 tablespoons butter

1½ cups dried green or brown lentils, rinsed and drained

1 14-ounce can beef broth or vegetable broth

1¼ cups water

¼ teaspoon ground black pepper

6 cups baby spinach, torn

Salt

2 tablespoons snipped fresh mint (optional)

1 In a large saucepan cook sweet pepper, onion, garlic, and curry powder in hot butter for 2 to 3 minutes or until vegetables are just tender.

2 Stir in lentils, broth, water, and black pepper. Bring to boiling; reduce heat. Simmer, covered, about 30 minutes or until lentils are tender and most of the liquid is absorbed.

3 Stir in spinach; cook about 2 minutes more or until spinach is wilted. Season to taste with salt and pepper. If desired, serve with mint. **Makes 6 servings**

Nutrition facts per serving: 163 cal., 4 g total fat (2 g sat. fat), 11 mg chol., 272 mg sodium, 23 g carb., 5 g dietary fiber, 9 g protein.

Indian Lentils and Rice

START TO FINISH: 20 MINUTES

1 tablespoon vegetable oil

½ cup chopped onion (1 medium)

2 teaspoons garam masala

2 cups bite-size cauliflower florets

½ cup bias-sliced carrot (1 medium)

1 cup water

1 17.3-ounce package refrigerated steamed lentils, or one 15-ounce can lentils, rinsed and drained*

1 8.8-ounce pouch cooked long grain rice

1 cup thawed frozen peas

⅓ cup golden raisins

Salt and ground black pepper

1 In an extra-large skillet heat oil over medium heat. Add onion and garam masala; cook about 5 minutes or until onion is tender. Add cauliflower, carrot, and the water. Bring to boiling; reduce heat. Simmer, covered, about 5 minutes or until tender.

2 Stir in lentils, rice, peas, and raisins; cook and stir until heated through and water is absorbed. Season to taste with salt and pepper. **Makes 4 to 6 servings**

Nutrition facts per serving: 373 cal., 6 g total fat (0 g sat. fat), 0 mg chol., 510 mg sodium, 65 g carb., 14 g dietary fiber, 17 g sugar, 17 g protein.

***Note:** If these are not available, in a large saucepan combine 8 ounces dried lentils and 2 ½ cups water. Bring to boiling; reduce heat. Simmer, covered, about 30 minutes or until tender.*

Butterut Squash–Red Lentil Dal with Fragrant Basmati Rice

PREP: 20 MINUTES   **COOK:** 15 MINUTES

2 teaspoons brown mustard seeds

3 tablespoons clarified butter (ghee)

1½ cups chopped onions (3 medium)

2 tablespoons grated fresh ginger

1 tablespoon garam masala

4 cloves garlic, minced

1 teaspoon ground cumin

¼ teaspoon cardamom seeds

6 cups water or vegetable broth

4 cups peeled and seeded butternut
   squash cut into 1-inch cubes

1½ cups dried red lentils

½ cup coarsely chopped fresh cilantro

½ teaspoon salt*

½ teaspoon ground black pepper

1 recipe Fragrant Basmati Rice

   Chopped fresh cilantro (optional)

1 In a large saucepan cook mustard seeds in hot ghee over medium heat about 1 minute or until seeds pops. Reduce heat to low. Add onions, ginger, garam masala, garlic, cumin, and cardamom seeds; cook about 2 minutes more or until fragrant.

2 Add the water, butternut squash, and lentils to saucepan. Bring to boiling; reduce heat. Simmer, uncovered, for 10 to 20 minutes or until squash is tender, stirring occasionally.

3 Add ½ cup cilantro, salt, and pepper. Scoop ¾ cup Fragrant Basmati Rice into individual serving bowls; top with lentil-squash mixture. If desired, sprinkle with additional cilantro. Serve immediately. **Makes 6 servings**

Nutrition facts per serving: 443 cal., 10 g total fat (0 g sat. fat), 0 mg chol., 414 mg sodium, 72 g carb., 19 g dietary fiber, 6 g sugar, 17 g protein.

Fragrant Basmati Rice: In a large skillet cook ½ cup chopped red sweet pepper (1 small); ½ cup chopped yellow sweet pepper (1 small); ½ cup chopped onion (1 medium); and 1 clove garlic, minced in 1 tablespoon of vegetable oil over medium heat about 10 minutes or until vegetables are tender, stirring frequently. Stir in 2 cups water, 1 cup white Basmati rice, and ½ teaspoon salt. Bring to boiling; reduce heat. Simmer, covered, about 15 minutes, or until rice is tender and liquid is absorbed.

***Note:** Omit salt if using vegetable broth.*

Kitchen Tip Ghee is a type of clarified butter widely used in Indian cooking. Clarified butter is butter that has had the milk solids removed so that just the golden butterfat is left. Ghee is different than the clarified butter (also called drawn butter) that you eat with lobster. It has been cooked longer to remove all moisture. The milk solids are brown or caramelized, which gives the ghee a rich, nutty taste. Look for it at Indian markets and health food stores.

Sweet Potato and Chickpea Coconut Curry

START TO FINISH: 30 MINUTES

½ cup chopped onion (1 medium)

½ cup chopped red sweet pepper (1 small)

1 tablespoon olive oil

2 cups ½-inch pieces peeled sweet potatoes

1 16-ounce can garbanzo beans (chickpeas), rinsed and drained

1 tablespoon curry powder

1 teaspoon ground cumin

½ teaspoon salt

¼ teaspoon ground cinnamon

1 14-ounce can chicken broth

⅓ cup unsweetened coconut milk

2 cups hot cooked rice or couscous

Snipped fresh cilantro

Lime wedges

1 In a large saucepan cook onion and sweet pepper in hot oil over medium heat for 5 to 7 minutes or until tender and lightly brown, stirring occasionally. Add sweet potato, garbanzo beans, curry powder, cumin, salt, and cinnamon; cook for 5 minutes more, stirring occasionally.

2 Add broth and coconut milk to saucepan. Bring to boiling; reduce heat. Simmer, uncovered, for 8 to 10 minutes or until potatoes are tender. Serve over rice. Garnish with cilantro and serve with lime wedges. **Makes 4 servings**

Nutrition facts per serving: 337 cal., 10 g total fat (5 g sat. fat), 1 mg chol., 1,134 mg sodium, 59 g carb., 9 g dietary fiber, 11 g protein.

Udon Noodle Bowl

START TO FINISH: 40 MINUTES

- 6 ounces udon (Japanese) noodles
- 1 tablespoon sesame oil (not toasted)
- 1 to 2 teaspoons grated fresh ginger
- 2 cloves garlic, minced
- 6 ounces shiitake mushrooms, stemmed and sliced
- 1 fresh serrano chile pepper, stem removed and thinly sliced*
- 1 teaspoon finely shredded orange zest
- 4 cups reduced-sodium chicken broth or vegetable broth
- ¼ cup sake or dry sherry
- 3 tablespoons reduced-sodium soy sauce
- 2 tablespoons orange juice
- 3 tablespoons miso paste
- 8 ounces firm silken tofu, cut into cubes
- 2 cups shredded napa cabbage
- 1 ounce enoki mushrooms, divided into small bunches (optional)
- ¼ cup coarsely shredded carrot
- ¼ cup sliced scallions (2)
- ½ cup fresh cilantro leaves

Kitchen Tip At between 4 and 8 millimeters wide, udon are the thickest of the Japanese noodles. They are white, made from wheat flour, and can be eaten hot or cold. Look for them at larger supermarkets and Asian markets.

1 Cook noodles according to package directions; drain.

2 Meanwhile, in a large saucepan heat oil over medium-high heat. Add ginger and garlic; cook and stir for 30 seconds. Add shiitake mushrooms and chile pepper; cook and stir for 2 minutes. Stir in orange zest.

3 Add broth and sake to mushroom mixture. Bring to boiling; reduce heat to medium low. Keep mixture at a simmer. Stir in soy sauce and orange juice.

4 In a small bowl stir together miso and about ½ cup warm broth mixture. Add miso mixture and tofu to broth mixture in saucepan.

5 When ready to serve, divide noodles among warmed large deep soup bowls. Top with cabbage, enoki mushrooms (if using), carrot, and scallions. Ladle hot broth mixture over noodles and top with cilantro leaves. **Makes 4 servings**

Nutrition facts per serving: 339 cal., 7 g total fat (1 g sat. fat), 0 mg chol., 1,548 mg sodium, 49 g carb., 6 g dietary fiber, 7 g sugar, 18 g protein.

*Note: *Because hot chile peppers contain volatile oils that can burn your skin and eyes, avoid contact with chiles as much as possible. When working with chile peppers, wear plastic or rubber gloves. If your bare hands do touch the chile peppers, wash your hands well with soap and water.*

Make-It-Mine Asian Bowl

PREP: 30 MINUTES   **COOK:** 15 MINUTES

Sauce ingredients, page 64

Meat, page 64

2 **eggs, lightly beaten**

1 **tablespoon milk**

1 **clove garlic, minced**

½ **teaspoon salt**

½ **teaspoon ground black pepper**

2 **cups panko (Japanese-style bread crumbs)**

2 **tablespoons vegetable oil**

2 **teaspoons vegetable oil**

Vegetables, page 64

Rice or noodles, page 64

Salt

1 In a small bowl stir together Sauce ingredients until well combined. Cover and chill until ready to serve. Bring to room temperature before serving.

2 Place meat, if using, between 2 sheets of plastic wrap and pound with the flat side of a meat mallet or with a rolling pin to ⅛-inch thickness.

3 In a medium bowl beat together eggs, milk, garlic, ½ teaspoon salt, and the pepper. Place panko in a shallow dish. Dip meat or eggplant in egg mixture, allowing excess to drip off. Dip in panko to coat completely. Transfer to a plate or tray until ready to cook.

4 In a large, deep heavy skillet heat 2 tablespoons oil over medium heat. Add meat or eggplant; cook for 3 to 4 minutes on each side until golden brown (if necessary, add more oil). Transfer to a wire rack set in a shallow baking pan. Cover and keep warm.

5 In same skillet heat 2 teaspoons oil over medium-high heat. Add Vegetables; cook and stir for 3 to 4 minutes or until vegetables are crisp-tender.

6 Add Rice or Noodle Additions; cook and stir until heated through. Season to taste with salt. Slice meat or eggplant into thin strips.

7 To serve, divide vegetable mixture among bowls. Top with sliced meat or eggplant. Top with some of the sauce; serve with remaining sauce. **Makes 4 to 6 servings**

SAUCE

Pork Katsu and Rice Bowl

- ¼ cup ketchup
- 2 tablespoons mirin, sake, or dry sherry
- 1 tablespoon reduced-sodium soy sauce
- 2 teaspoons Chinese-style hot mustard
- 1 teaspoon sugar

Chicken Katsu and Rice Noodle Bowl

- 1 large carrot, coarsely shredded
- ¼ of a seedless cucumber, halved lengthwise and very thinly sliced
- ¼ cup thinly sliced scallions (2)
- 3 tablespoons rice vinegar
- 2 tablespoons water
- 2 teaspoons sugar

Beef Katsu and Soba Noodle Bowl

- 3 tablespoons warm water
- 2 tablespoons miso paste
- 2 teaspoons Chinese-style hot mustard
- 1 teaspoon toasted sesame oil
- 1 teaspoon grated fresh ginger

Eggplant Katsu and Egg Noodle Bowl

- 2 tablespoons Asian chili sauce
- 2 tablespoons water
- 2 tablespoons reduced-sodium soy sauce
- 1 tablespoon rice vinegar
- 2 teaspoons sugar

VEGETABLES

Pork Katsu and Rice Bowl

- 1 cup fresh or thawed frozen peas
- 4 ounces shiitake mushrooms, stemmed and thinly sliced
- 2 cloves garlic, minced

Chicken Katsu and Rice Noodle Bowl

- 2 cups snow peas, diagonally sliced in half crosswise
- 2 shallots, thinly sliced

Beef Katsu and Soba Noodle Bowl

- 1 small red sweet pepper, cut into thin bite-size strips
- ¼ of a small red onion, thinly sliced

Eggplant Katsu and Egg Noodle Bowl

- 1 small yellow sweet pepper, cut into thin bite-size strips
- ¼ cup sliced scallions (2)
- 1 cup very small broccoli florets

RICE OR NOODLE ADDITIONS

Pork Katsu and Rice Bowl

3 cups cooked long grain rice, cooled and broken up (leftovers work well)

1½ cups finely shredded cabbage

¼ cup reduced-sodium chicken broth

Chicken Katsu and Rice Noodle Bowl

4 cups cooked rice noodles, rinsed and drained

Beef Katsu and Soba Noodle Bowl

4 cups cooked soba noodles, rinsed and drained

4 cups baby spinach

1 tablespoon toasted sesame seeds

Eggplant Katsu and Egg Noodle Bowl

4 cups cooked Asian-style egg noodles, rinsed and drained

2 eggs, lightly beaten and scrambled

Bowl Bit *Katsu* refers to a Japanese method of pounding a piece of meat flat, then breading it, frying it, and serving it with sides of crispy vegetables and/or rice. The original katsu was *tonkatsu*, a crisp-fried pork cutlet. This dish was developed during a historical period from the mid-1800s to the early 1900s, when Japan was beginning to experience Western influence. *Tonkatsu* is thought to have originated from Austrian *schnitzel*—thin, breaded and fried scallops of veal. In this customizable recipe, the katsu method of cooking is applied to pork, beef, chicken—even eggplant.

The European bowl

Cappellini

Spaghetti

Linguine

Pappardelle

Rigatoni

Penne/
Mostaccioli

Fettuccine

Mafalda

Spaetzle

Orecchiette

Penne

Ziti

Orzo

Couscous

Fine egg noodle

Medium
egg noodle

Wide
egg noodle

Extra wide
egg noodle

European Noodles

1. Capellini: Thin strands of Italian wheat pasta that are slightly thicker than what is called angel hair pasta. Sold straight or in nests, they are usually served in broth or with thin or delicate sauces.

2. Spaghetti: The most popular pasta variety, the name means "little strings" in Italian. Spaghetti is best with light tomato or cream sauces.

3. Linguine: Narrow ribbons of pasta that are often served with clams or shrimp. The name means "little tongues" in Italian.

4. Fettuccine: Slightly wider than linguine, these noodles (literally "little ribbons") go well with cream sauces.

5. Mafalda: The ruffled edges on these long, flat, and wide noodles make them resemble a narrow lasagne noodle. They hold up well to thick, meaty sauces.

6. Pappardelle: These very thick wide ribbons of pasta—about ⅝ inch wide—come both straight and in nests. Pappardelle (literally "gulp down") pairs well with hearty meat sauces.

7. Rigatoni: These large, grooved pasta tubes are substantial and toothsome. Like ziti, they are often paired with hearty vegetable or meat sauces or baked into casseroles. The ridges help to hold and absorb the sauce.

8. Penne: Literally "pens" or "quills" in Italian, the diagonal cut on these pasta tubes helps to scoop the sauce inside. Penne is quite versatile and can be tossed with sauce, baked into a casserole, or used in pasta salad.

9. Spaetzle: Translated from German, the name for this cross between a dumpling and a noodle means "little sparrow." These little pillows made from wheat flour, egg, and milk are eaten in Germany and Austria. To make spaetzle, the dough is often forced through a large-holed colander into a pot of boiling water.

10. Orecchiette: These "little ears" of pasta are shaped like tiny bowls or disks. They work well with moderately chunky sauces.

11. Orzo: This rice-shaped pasta is best served as a side dish to roasted or grilled meats, stirred into soup, or tossed in a pasta salad.

12. Ziti: These smooth, hollow tubes of pasta ("bridegrooms" in Italian) range from 2 to 12 inches long. The shorter versions, called cut ziti, are more common in American supermarkets. They go well with hearty meat sauces and are often baked into casseroles.

13. Couscous: These tiny grains of wheat pasta originated in North Africa and migrated north to Sicily. Precooked or instant couscous is the most common type available. It requires no cooking. It's simply added to boiling water, taken off the heat, and is ready to eat in about 5 minutes.

14. Fine egg noodles: Made with eggs and wheat, egg noodles come in a variety of shapes and sizes (see #14, #15, and #16). Fine egg noodles are best used in soups.

15. Medium egg noodles: This versatile noodle works well in soups and casseroles. Buttered, they can be served as accompaniments to European dishes such as French Coq au Vin or Russian Beef Stroganoff. They also show up in many American dishes, including Chicken and Noodles and Beef and Noodles.

16. Wide egg noodles: This size works well in casseroles and noodle bakes.

17. Extra-wide egg noodles: This size is hearty enough to stand up to meaty sauces. They, like wide noodles, also work well in casseroles and noodle bakes.

Meaty Merlot Ragu with Pappardelle

PREP: 40 MINUTES   **COOK:** 20 MINUTES

3 tablespoons olive oil

8 ounces cremini mushrooms, chopped

1 cup chopped onion (1 large)

¾ cup chopped carrot

½ cup finely chopped red or green
   sweet pepper (1 small)

3 ounces pancetta, chopped

3 cloves garlic, minced

1 teaspoon snipped fresh rosemary

½ teaspoon fennel seeds

1 pound lean ground beef

8 ounces bulk Italian sausage

1 15-ounce can tomato sauce

1 cup Merlot or other dry red wine

1 tablespoon balsamic vinegar

1 pound dried pappardelle pasta

   Shredded Parmigiano-Reggiano
   or Asiago cheese

1 In a 4-quart Dutch oven heat 2 tablespoons of the oil over medium-high heat. Add mushrooms, onion, carrot, sweet pepper, pancetta, garlic, rosemary, and fennel seeds; cook and stir until mushrooms are tender and liquid is evaporated. Remove vegetable mixture from Dutch oven.

2 Add the remaining 1 tablespoon oil to Dutch oven; heat over medium-high heat. Add ground beef and sausage; cook and stir until meat is brown, using a wooden spoon to break up meat as it cooks.

3 Return cooked vegetables to Dutch oven. Stir in tomato sauce, wine, and vinegar. Bring to boiling; reduce heat. Simmer, uncovered, about 20 minutes or until slightly thickened.

4 Meanwhile, cook pasta according to package directions; drain. Serve meat mixture over hot cooked pasta. Sprinkle with cheese. **Makes 8 servings**

Nutrition facts per serving: 603 cal., 30 g total fat (10 g sat. fat), 119 mg chol., 827 mg sodium, 49 g carb., 4 g dietary fiber, 6 g sugar, 28 g protein.

Carbonnade of Beef and Vegetables

PREP: 15 MINUTES   **COOK:** 1 HOUR 15 MINUTES

4   slices bacon

2   pounds boneless beef top round steak, cut into 1-inch cubes

3   large leeks or medium onions, sliced

2   12-ounce bottles dark beer or ale

¼   cup red wine vinegar

3   tablespoons packed brown sugar

2   tablespoons instant beef bouillon granules

2   teaspoons dried thyme, crushed

½   teaspoon ground black pepper

4   cloves garlic, minced

1½   pounds carrots and/or parsnips, bias-sliced into ½-inch pieces

¼   cup water

¼   cup all-purpose flour

Hot cooked wide noodles (optional)

1 In a 4-quart Dutch oven cook bacon over medium heat until crisp. Remove bacon; reserve drippings in Dutch oven. Drain bacon on paper towels. Crumble bacon; set aside.

2 Brown meat cubes, half at a time, in reserved bacon drippings; drain off fat. Return all browned meat to Dutch oven. Add leeks, beer, vinegar, brown sugar, bouillon granules, thyme, pepper, and garlic. Bring to boiling; reduce heat. Simmer, covered, for 45 minutes, stirring occasionally. Add carrots. Return to boiling; reduce heat. Simmer, covered, for 30 to 35 minutes more or until meat and vegetables are tender.

3 In a screw-top jar combine the water and flour. Cover and shake until smooth. Add flour mixture to Dutch oven; cook and stir over medium heat until thickened and bubbly. Cook and stir for 1 minute more. Stir in bacon. If desired, serve beef and vegetable mixture over noodles. **Makes 8 servings**

Nutrition facts per serving: 390 cal., 6 g total fat (2 g sat. fat), 94 mg chol., 813 mg sodium, 42 g carb., 4 g dietary fiber, 33 g protein.

Bowl Bit Belgium is rightly famous for its delicious beers and ales, and there are many ways to enjoy them other than sipped from a glass. The traditional Belgian dish *carbonnade à la flamande* is a hearty stew of beef simmered with bacon, onions, brown sugar, and of course, Belgian beer. The dark beer in this recipe lends gives the stew rich flavor and creates a beautiful deep brown sauce. If you can find a Belgian dark beer (Chimay Blue is the most widely available), give it a try in this recipe.

Polenta Beef Stew

PREP: 25 MINUTES   **COOK:** 2 HOURS

¼ cup all-purpose flour

1 teaspoon garlic powder

1 teaspoon dried thyme, crushed

1 teaspoon dried basil, crushed

½ teaspoon salt

½ teaspoon ground black pepper

2 pounds boneless beef chuck steak, cut into 1-inch cubes

2 tablespoons olive oil

½ cup chopped onion (1 medium)

1 teaspoon snipped fresh rosemary, or ¼ teaspoon dried rosemary, crushed

6 cloves garlic, minced

1 14-ounce can beef broth

1½ cups dry red wine

8 ounces boiling onions, peeled

5 medium carrots, cut into 1-inch pieces

½ cup snipped fresh flat-leaf parsley

¼ cup tomato paste

1 recipe Polenta

   Fresh parsley sprigs (optional)

1 Combine flour, garlic powder, thyme, basil, salt, and pepper in a resealable plastic bag. Add meat cubes, a few at a time, shaking to coat. In a 4- to 5-quart Dutch oven heat oil over medium heat. Add beef cubes, half at a time; cook and stir until beef is brown. Drain off fat. Return all beef to Dutch oven. Add onion, dried rosemary (if using), and garlic; cook and stir for 3 to 4 minutes. Stir in broth and wine. Bring to boiling; reduce heat. Simmer, covered, for 1½ hours.

2 Stir in boiling onions and carrots. Bring to boiling; reduce heat. Simmer, covered, about 30 minutes more or until meat and vegetables are tender.

3 Stir in snipped parsley, tomato paste, and fresh rosemary (if using). Serve with Polenta. If desired, garnish each serving with parsley sprigs. **Makes 8 servings**

Nutrition facts per serving: 508 cal., 26 g total fat (10 g sat. fat), 88 mg chol., 736 mg sodium, 32 g carb., 4 g dietary fiber, 9 g sugar, 29 g protein.

Polenta: In a large saucepan bring 3 cups milk just to a simmer over medium heat. In a medium bowl combine 1 cup cornmeal, 1 cup water, and 1 teaspoon salt. Stir cornmeal mixture slowly into hot milk. Cook and stir until mixture comes to a boil; reduce heat to low. Cook for 10 to 15 minutes or until mixture is very thick, stirring occasionally. (If mixture is too thick, stir in additional milk.) Stir in 2 tablespoons butter until melted.

French-Style Beef Stew

PREP: 35 MINUTES   **COOK:** 1 HOUR 45 MINUTES

1 tablespoon olive oil

1 pound boneless beef top round steak, cut into 1-inch cubes

½ cup chopped onion (1 medium)

1 cup dry white wine

2 cups water

1 teaspoon dried herbes de Provence, crushed

¼ teaspoon salt

¼ teaspoon ground black pepper

16 peeled baby carrots

8 tiny new potatoes, halved or quartered

8 pearl onions, peeled

1 large tomato, peeled, seeded, and chopped

¼ cup pitted niçoise or kalamata olives

2 tablespoons capers, drained

8 ounces steamed haricots verts or small green beans

1 tablespoon snipped fresh flat-leaf parsley

1 In a 4-quart Dutch oven heat oil over medium heat. Add beef cubes and chopped onion, half at a time; cook and stir until beef is brown. Drain off fat. Return all beef mixture to Dutch oven.

2 Add wine to Dutch oven; cook and stir over medium heat, scraping up brown bits in bottom of Dutch oven. Add water, herbes de Provence, salt, and pepper. Bring to boiling; reduce heat. Simmer, covered, about 1¼ hours or until meat is nearly tender. Add carrots, potatoes, and pearl onions. Return to boiling; reduce heat. Simmer, covered, about 30 minutes more or until meat and vegetables are tender. Stir in tomato, olives, and capers; heat through.

3 Place haricots verts in shallow soup bowls; top with stew. Sprinkle each serving with parsley. **Makes 4 servings**

Nutrition facts per serving: 377 cal., 10 g total fat (2 g sat. fat), 72 mg chol., 399 mg sodium, 31 g carb., 5 g dietary fiber, 31 g protein.

Beef Stroganoff

START TO FINISH: 30 MINUTES

- 3 **cups packaged dried wide noodles**
- 3 **cups broccoli spears (12 ounces)**
- ½ **cup light sour cream**
- 1½ **teaspoons prepared horseradish**
- ½ **teaspoon snipped fresh dill**
- 1 **pound beef rib-eye steak**
- 1 **small onion, cut into ½-inch slices**
- ½ **teaspoon bottled minced garlic**
- 1 **tablespoon vegetable oil**
- 4 **teaspoons all-purpose flour**
- ½ **teaspoon ground black pepper**
- 1 **14-ounce can beef broth**
- 3 **tablespoons tomato paste**
- 1 **teaspoon Worcestershire sauce**
  Snipped fresh dill (optional)

Bowl Bit Though this dish has become quite Americanized, its first known reference comes from a classic Russian cookbook from 1861. It was likely named for a member of the large and important Stroganov family. That first recipe was simply lightly floured beef cubes that were sautéed, sauced with mustard and broth, and finished with a little sour cream. Since then, hundreds of variations have cropped up all over the world—some with rice, some with noodles, some with mushrooms and other vegetables—such as this one that includes fresh broccoli.

1 Cook noodles according to package directions, adding broccoli for the last 5 minutes of cooking. Drain; return noodles and broccoli to pan.

2 Meanwhile, in a small bowl stir together sour cream, horseradish, and ½ teaspoon dill; cover and chill until serving time.

3 Trim fat from beef. Cut beef into bite-size strips. In a large skillet cook half of the beef and all of the onion and garlic in hot oil until onion is tender and beef is of desired doneness. Remove from skillet. Add remaining beef; cook and stir until beef is of desired doneness. Return all meat to skillet; sprinkle flour and pepper over meat. Stir to coat.

4 Stir in broth, tomato paste, and Worcestershire sauce; cook and stir until mixture is thickened and bubbly. Cook and stir 1 minute more. Divide noodle-broccoli mixture among bowls. Spoon beef mixture on top of noodle mixture. Top with one or two spoonfuls of the sour cream mixture. If desired, garnish with additional dill. **Makes 4 servings**

Nutrition facts per serving: 368 cal., 15 g total fat (5 g sat. fat), 81 mg chol., 454 mg sodium, 32 g carb., 4 g dietary fiber, 4 g sugar, 29 g protein.

Poutine

PREP: 30 MINUTES   **COOK:** 1 HOUR 10 MINUTES   **COOL:** 10 MINUTES

3 tablespoons all-purpose flour

1 teaspoon smoked paprika

½ teaspoon salt

¼ teaspoon ground black pepper

8 ounces boneless beef chuck, cut into 1½-inch pieces

1 tablespoon canola oil

1 tablespoon butter

½ cup chopped onion (1 medium)

1 14-ounce can reduced-sodium beef broth

1 cup water

2 teaspoons canola oil

8 ounces white mushrooms, sliced

1 recipe French Fries, or ½ of a 28-ounce package frozen French-fried shoestring potatoes, cooked according to package directions

1½ cups cheese curds, broken up

Bowl Bit Technically, this is a French-Canadian diner food, but its French name (and utter deliciousness) merits its inclusion in this book. Poutine (poo-TEEN) is very much like American gravy fries—with the addition of fresh cheese curds that melt slightly when topped with the hot gravy. The name is likely a French twist on the English word *pudding*.

1 In a medium bowl combine flour, paprika, salt, and pepper; reserve half of the mixture. Add beef to remaining mixture and toss to coat.

2 In a large heavy saucepan heat 1 tablespoon oil and the butter over medium-high heat. Shake excess flour from beef; reserve any remaining flour mixture. Add beef to pan; cook for 6 to 8 minutes or until brown, turning occasionally.

3 Add onion to pan; cook and stir for 2 minutes. Sprinkle remaining flour mixture used to coat beef over meat and onions; cook and stir for 2 minutes more. Add broth and ¾ cup of the water to pan. Bring to boiling, stirring to scrape up any brown bits from bottom of pan. Reduce heat to low; cover and simmer for 1 to 1½ hours or until meat is very tender, stirring occasionally.

4 With a slotted spoon transfer beef to a large heatproof bowl and cool for 10 minutes. Using 2 forks, shred beef into small pieces. Pour liquid in pan over beef.

5 In the same pan heat 2 teaspoons oil over medium-high heat. Add mushrooms; cook and stir for 3 to 4 minutes or just until tender. Add beef mixture. Combine reserved flour mixture and the reserved ¼ cup water. Stir into beef mixture; cook and stir until thickened and bubbly. Cook for 1 minute more. Cover and keep warm until serving time.

6 To serve, divide hot French Fries among bowls. Top with warm beef mixture and cheese curds. Serve immediately. **Makes 4 servings**

Nutrition facts per serving: 759 cal., 49 g total fat (18 g sat. fat), 97 mg chol., 1,007 mg sodium, 50 g carb., 6 g dietary fiber, 4 g sugar, 31 g protein.

French Fries: Cut 2 pounds russet potatoes into ⅓-inch-thick strips. Soak in ice-cold water for 45 to 60 minutes; drain and dry thoroughly with paper towels. Heat 2 quarts vegetable oil in a fryer or deep pot to 340°F. Fry potatoes in batches for 3 minutes or until fork-tender; remove and drain on a wire rack over a baking pan. Bring oil to 365°F and fry potatoes again in batches for 3 to 5 minutes or until crisp and golden brown. Return fries to wire rack and season with salt and ground black pepper.

Beef Bourguignonne

PREP: 40 MINUTES   **COOK:** 1 HOUR 15 MINUTES

- 1 **pound boneless beef chuck roast, cut into ¾-inch cubes**
- 2 **tablespoons vegetable oil**
- 1 **cup chopped onion (1 large)**
- 1 **clove garlic, minced**
- 1½ **cups Burgundy wine**
- ¾ **cup beef broth**
- 1 **teaspoon dried thyme, crushed**
- ¾ **teaspoon dried marjoram, crushed**
- 2 **bay leaves**
- ½ **teaspoon salt**
- ¼ **teaspoon ground black pepper**
- 3 **cups whole mushrooms**
- 4 **medium carrots, cut into ¾-inch pieces**
- 8 **ounces pearl onions, or 2 cups frozen small whole onions**
- 2 **tablespoons all-purpose flour**
- ¼ **cup water**
- 3 **cups hot cooked noodles or mashed potatoes**
- 2 **slices bacon, crisp-cooked, drained, and crumbled**
- 1 **tablespoon snipped fresh parsley**

1 In a large pot cook half of the meat in 1 tablespoon of the hot oil until meat is brown; remove meat from pan. Add remaining oil and meat, chopped onion, and garlic to pot; cook until meat is brown and onion is tender. Drain off fat. Return all meat to pot.

2 Stir in wine, broth, thyme, marjoram, bay leaves, salt, and pepper. Bring to boiling; reduce heat. Simmer, covered, for 45 minutes, stirring occasionally. Add mushrooms, carrots, and pearl onions. Return to boiling; reduce heat. Simmer, covered, for 25 to 30 minutes more or until vegetables are tender, stirring occasionally. Remove and discard bay leaves.

3 Combine flour and water. Stir flour mixture into meat mixture; cook and stir until thickened and bubbly. Cook and stir for 1 minute more. Serve with noodles. Top with bacon and parsley. **Makes 6 servings**

Nutrition facts per serving: 430 cal., 19 g total fat (6 g sat. fat), 66 mg chol., 444 mg sodium, 35 g carb., 4 g dietary fiber, 6 g sugar, 19 g protein.

German Meatballs with Spaetzle

PREP: 20 MINUTES   **COOK:** 25 MINUTES

1   egg, lightly beaten

¼   cup milk

¼   cup fine dry bread crumbs

1   tablespoon snipped fresh parsley

½   teaspoon salt

     Pinch ground black pepper

1   pound ground beef

1⅓ cups beef broth

1   4-ounce can mushroom pieces and stems, drained

½   cup chopped onion (1 medium)

1   8-ounce carton sour cream

2   tablespoons all-purpose flour

½   to 1 teaspoon caraway seeds

2   cups all-purpose flour

1   teaspoon salt

2   eggs, lightly beaten

1   cup milk

     Snipped fresh parsley (optional)

1 For meatballs, in a large bowl combine the 1 egg, ¼ cup milk, bread crumbs, 1 tablespoon parsley, ½ teaspoon salt, and pepper. Add ground beef; mix well. Shape mixture into twenty-four 1½-inch meatballs.

2 In a large nonstick skillet brown meatballs over medium-high heat; drain off fat. Add beef broth, mushrooms, and onion. Bring to boiling; reduce heat. Simmer, covered, about 20 minutes or until meatballs are done (an instant-read thermometer inserted into meatballs registers 160°F). In a small bowl combine sour cream, 2 tablespoons flour, and caraway seeds. Stir into broth; cook and stir until mixture is thickened and bubbly. Cook and stir for 1 minute more.

3 Meanwhile, for spaetzle, in a medium bowl, combine 2 cups flour and 1 teaspoon salt. Add the 2 eggs and 1 cup milk; beat well with wooden spoon. Let rest for 5 to 10 minutes. Bring a large saucepan of salted water to boiling. Holding a coarse-sieved colander or the basket for a deep-fat fryer over the pan of rapidly boiling water, pour batter into colander. Press batter through colander with back of wooden spoon. Cook and stir for 5 minutes; drain. Serve meatballs with spaetzle. If desired, sprinkle with parsley. **Makes 6 servings**

Nutrition facts per serving: 489 cal., 23 g total fat (10 g sat. fat), 180 mg chol., 1,116 mg sodium, 43 g carb., 2 g dietary fiber, 5 g sugar, 26 g protein.

Country French Cassoulet

PREP: 40 MINUTES   **COOK:** 3 HOURS 20 MINUTES   **STAND:** 15 MINUTES   **OVEN:** 325°F/400°F

1½ pounds dried Great Northern beans (3¾ cups)

8 cups water

5 fresh parsley sprigs

3 celery leaves

2 fresh thyme sprigs

2 bay leaves

5 whole cloves

½ teaspoon whole black peppercorns

8 ounces unsmoked bacon, ham, or pancetta

1 medium onion, cut in half

½ cup coarsely chopped carrot (1 medium)

10 cloves garlic

10 cups water

4 cups beef broth, or 2 cups duck and veal demi-glace dissolved in 2 cups water

3 cups peeled, seeded, and chopped tomatoes (6 medium)

½ cup chopped onion (1 medium)

Pinch ground black pepper

4 duck legs confit

1 pound garlic sausage, halved crosswise or cut into large slices

Kosher salt, sea salt, or salt

1 Rinse beans. In a 4-quart Dutch oven combine beans and the 8 cups water. Bring to boiling; reduce heat. Simmer, uncovered, for 2 minutes. Remove from heat. Cover and let stand for 1 hour. (Or place beans in the water in Dutch oven. Cover and let soak in a cool place for 6 to 8 hours or overnight.) Drain and return beans to Dutch oven.

2 For bouquet garni, place parsley, celery leaves, thyme, bay leaves, cloves, and peppercorns in the center of a double-thick, 6-inch square of 100-percent-cotton cheesecloth. Bring up corners and tie closed with clean kitchen string. Add bouquet garni, bacon, onion halves, carrot, garlic, and the 10 cups water to beans in Dutch oven. Bring to boiling; reduce heat. Simmer, covered, about 1 hour or just until beans are tender, stirring often. Drain; remove and discard onion halves and bouquet garni. Return bean mixture to Dutch oven. Add broth, tomatoes, ½ cup chopped onion, and pinch pepper; bring to boiling.

3 Meanwhile preheat oven to 325°F. Remove duck meat from bones or cut each duck leg in half at the joint. Remove half of the bean mixture from the Dutch oven. Add duck and sausage; cover with the removed bean mixture. Bake, covered, about 2 hours or bubbly.

4 Increase oven temperature to 400°F. Bake, uncovered, about 20 minutes more or until top is brown. Remove from oven; let casserole stand for 15 minutes before serving. Season to taste with salt and additional pepper. **Makes 8 servings**

Nutrition facts per serving: 648 cal., 24 g total fat (8 g sat. fat), 102 mg chol., 1,359 mg sodium, 63 g carb., 20 g dietary fiber, 7 g sugar, 45 g protein.

Bowl Bit To the French, this rich, slow-cooked dish of white beans and meats defines comfort food. Named for its cooking vessel—a deep, round earthenware pot with slanted sides called a *cassole*—and originating in the south of France, true cassoulet always contains confit (kawn-FEE). Confit is a process of salt-curing a piece of meat and then poaching it in its own fat. You can find duck legs confit at specialty food stores and online.

Cassoulet-Style Lamb Stew

PREP: 2 HOURS   **COOK:** 1 HOUR 45 MINUTES

- 8 ounces dried navy beans
- 6½ cups water
- 1 tablespoon olive oil or vegetable oil
- 1 to 1½ pounds meaty lamb shanks
- 1 cup chopped celery (2 stalks)
- 1 cup peeled and coarsely chopped potato
- ½ cup coarsely chopped carrot
- ½ cup peeled and coarsely chopped parsnip (1 medium)
- 2 cloves garlic, minced
- 1½ cups sliced mushrooms
- ⅔ cup dried black-eyed peas, rinsed and drained
- ¼ cup dry red wine or beef broth
- 1¼ teaspoons salt
- 1 tablespoon snipped fresh thyme, or 1 teaspoon dried thyme, crushed
- 2 teaspoons snipped fresh rosemary, or ½ teaspoon dried rosemary, crushed
- ¼ teaspoon ground black pepper
- 1 14.5-ounce can diced tomatoes, undrained

  Fresh rosemary or thyme sprigs (optional)

1 Rinse beans. In a Dutch oven combine beans and 3 cups of the water. Bring to boiling; reduce heat. Simmer, uncovered, for 2 minutes. Remove from heat. Cover and let stand for 1 hour. (Or, place beans in water in a Dutch oven. Cover and let stand in a cool place for 6 to 8 hours or overnight.) Drain and rinse beans.

2 In a 4- to 5-quart Dutch oven heat oil over medium-high heat. Add lamb shanks; cook until brown. Add celery, potato, carrot, parsnip, and garlic; cook and stir for 5 minutes. Add mushrooms, black-eyed peas, wine, salt, dried thyme and dried rosemary (if using), pepper, beans, and the remaining water to Dutch oven. Bring to boiling; reduce heat. Simmer, covered, about 1½ hours or until the beans and peas are tender.

3 Remove lamb shanks from Dutch oven. When cool enough to handle, remove meat from bones. Discard bones. Chop meat. Return meat to Dutch oven. Add tomatoes and fresh snipped thyme and rosemary (if using). Return to boiling; reduce heat. Simmer, covered, for 15 minutes more. If desired, garnish each serving with rosemary or thyme sprigs. **Makes 6 servings**

Nutrition facts per serving: 310 cal., 8 g total fat (2 g sat. fat), 35 mg chol., 654 mg sodium, 39 g carb., 12 g dietary fiber, 20 g protein.

Choucroute Garni

PREP: 25 MINUTES   BAKE: 1 HOUR   OVEN: 375°F

 4 slices bacon, chopped

 1 large onion, thinly sliced and separated into rings

 4 cloves garlic, minced

 1 tablespoon vegetable oil

 6 pork loin rib chops, cut ¾ inch thick (about 2½ pounds)

 1 2-pound package refrigerated sauerkraut

 4 medium potatoes, peeled and cut into 1- to 2-inch pieces

12 ounces smoked sausage, cut into 1-inch pieces

 ¾ cup dry white wine or chicken broth

 ¾ cup chicken broth

 1 teaspoon juniper berries

 2 bay leaves

    Fresh rosemary sprigs (optional)

1 Preheat oven to 375°F. In an 8-quart Dutch oven cook bacon over medium heat until crisp. Add onion; cook and stir for 8 minutes. Add garlic; cook and stir for 1 minute. Drain off fat.

2 Meanwhile, in a large heavy skillet heat vegetable oil over medium-high heat. Season chops with salt and pepper. Brown chops in hot oil for 3 minutes per side.

3 Drain sauerkraut; rinse well. Squeeze excess liquid from sauerkraut; add to onion mixture. Stir in potatoes, sausage, wine, broth, juniper berries, and bay leaves. Bring to boiling; remove from heat. Place chops on top of sauerkraut.

4 Bake, covered, about 1 hour or until pork is no longer pink and potatoes are tender. To serve, remove and discard bay leaves. Arrange sauerkraut mixture in serving bowls; top with chops. If desired, garnish with rosemary sprigs. **Makes 6 servings**

Nutrition facts per serving: 565 cal., 30 g total fat (10 g sat. fat), 104 mg chol., 1,865 mg sodium, 24 g carb., 6 g dietary fiber, 42 g protein.

Spaghetti alla Carbonara

START TO FINISH: 40 MINUTES

12 ounces dried spaghetti

6 ounces pancetta, finely chopped

½ cup chopped onion (1 medium)

2 cloves garlic, minced

¼ cup dry white wine

2 pasteurized egg yolks, or ¼ cup refrigerated or frozen egg product, thawed

¼ cup whipping cream

¾ cup finely shredded Parmigiano-Reggiano cheese (3 ounces)

¼ cup finely shredded Pecorino Romano cheese (1 ounce)

½ teaspoon ground black pepper

½ teaspoon crushed red pepper

1 cup thawed frozen peas

¼ cup finely chopped bottled roasted red sweet pepper

1 In a large pot cook pasta according to package directions; drain, reserving ¼ cup pasta water. Return pasta to pan; keep warm.

2 Meanwhile, in a large skillet cook and stir pancetta over medium heat until crisp. Using a slotted spoon, transfer pancetta to paper towel–lined plate.

3 Add onion and garlic to hot drippings in skillet; cook and stir over medium heat about 5 minutes or until onion is tender. Remove skillet from heat; carefully add wine. Return skillet to heat. Bring wine to boiling; reduce heat. Simmer, uncovered, about 3 minutes or until most of the wine evaporates.

4 In a small bowl combine egg yolks and whipping cream. Stir in cheeses, black pepper, and crushed red pepper.

5 Add spaghetti and reserved pasta water to onion mixture in skillet; toss gently over medium heat for 1 to 2 minutes or until coated. Remove from heat; add egg mixture, peas, roasted sweet pepper, and reserved pancetta. Toss well to coat. Serve immediately. **Makes 6 servings**

Nutrition facts per serving: 460 cal., 19 g total fat (9 g sat. fat), 116 mg chol., 784 mg sodium, 49 g carb., 3 g dietary fiber, 4 g sugar, 19 g protein.

Bowl Bit One story of the origins of this bacon-and-egg-sauced pasta dish claims that during World War II, food shortages were so severe after the liberation of Rome that many locals received rations of powdered milk and bacon from American troops, from which they made this dish. This version uses pancetta—a type of Italian bacon that is cured but not smoked.

Ragu d'Agnello

PREP: 25 MINUTES   **COOK:** 40 MINUTES

½ cup chopped onion (1 medium)

½ cup chopped carrot (1 medium)

2 cloves garlic, minced

⅛ teaspoon crushed red pepper

1 tablespoon olive oil

1 pound ground lamb

½ teaspoon salt

¼ teaspoon ground black pepper

½ cup dry white wine

2 14.5-ounce cans diced tomatoes, undrained

1 teaspoon snipped fresh rosemary

1 teaspoon snipped fresh thyme

2 cups dried orzo (12 ounces), cooked

   Finely shredded Pecorino Romano cheese (optional)

1 In a large saucepan cook onion, carrot, garlic, and crushed red pepper in hot oil over medium heat for 5 minutes or until tender, stirring frequently. Add lamb, salt, and pepper; cook about 10 minutes or until lamb is brown, stirring to break up lamb. Drain off fat.

2 Add wine; cook, uncovered, about 5 minutes or until nearly evaporated, stirring occasionally. Stir in tomatoes, rosemary, and thyme. Bring to boiling; reduce heat. Simmer, uncovered, about 20 minutes or until desired consistency, stirring occasionally. Serve over hot cooked orzo. If desired, sprinkle with cheese. **Makes 4 servings**

Nutrition facts per serving: 658 cal., 20 g total fat (7 g sat. fat), 76 mg chol., 707 mg sodium, 78 g carb., 4 g dietary fiber, 10 g sugar, 32 g protein.

Bowl Bit *Agnello* simply means "lamb" in Italian. This rich, tomatoey sauce with ground lamb, white wine, and fresh rosemary and thyme is ladled over orzo.

Irish Stew

PREP: 25 MINUTES   **COOK:** 1 HOUR 16 MINUTES

1 pound boneless lamb or boneless beef chuck roast, cut into ¾-inch pieces

4 cups beef broth

2 medium onions, cut into wedges

¼ teaspoon ground black pepper

1 bay leaf

4 medium potatoes (1½ pounds), peeled and quartered

6 medium carrots, sliced ½ inch thick

½ teaspoon dried thyme, crushed

¼ teaspoon dried basil, crushed

½ cup water

¼ cup all-purpose flour

Salt and ground black pepper

1 In a large saucepan combine lamb, beef broth, onions, ¼ teaspoon pepper, and bay leaf. Bring to boiling; reduce heat. Simmer, covered, for 45 minutes. Skim off fat.

2 Add potatoes, carrots, thyme, and basil. Bring to boiling; reduce heat. Simmer, covered, for 30 to 35 minutes more or until vegetables are tender.

3 Combine water and flour. Stir into the stew; cook and stir until thickened and bubbly. Cook and stir for 1 minute more. Season to taste with salt and additional pepper. Remove and discard bay leaf before serving. **Makes 6 servings**

Nutrition facts per serving: 230 cal., 3 g total fat (1 g sat. fat), 48 mg chol., 649 mg sodium, 30 g carb., 4 g dietary fiber, 20 g protein.

Osso Buco Milan-Style

PREP: 25 MINUTES **COOK:** 1 HOUR 30 MINUTES **OVEN:** 350°F

¼ **cup all-purpose flour**

½ **teaspoon salt**

½ **teaspoon ground black pepper**

2 **to 2½ pounds veal shank cross-cuts (about four 2-inch-thick pieces)**

¼ **cup extra-virgin olive oil**

1 **cup chopped onion (1 large)**

½ **cup chopped carrot (1 medium)**

1 **tablespoon minced garlic**

3 **tablespoons tomato paste**

¾ **cup dry white or red wine**

4 **cups reduced-sodium beef broth**

1 **recipe Orzo Risotto**

1 **recipe Gremolata**

1 Preheat oven to 350°F. Combine flour, salt, and pepper in a resealable plastic bag. Add veal shanks, shake gently to coat. Remove shanks from bag, shaking off excess flour.

2 In a large Dutch oven cook shanks in hot oil for 10 to 12 minutes or until brown on all sides, turning occasionally. Transfer shanks to a platter; cover loosely with foil. Set aside.

3 Add onion, carrot, and garlic to Dutch oven; cook and stir for 8 to 10 minutes or until onion is golden brown. Add tomato paste; cook and stir for 2 to 3 minutes or until tomato paste turns brownish orange. Stir in wine.

4 Transfer shanks and any cooking liquid on platter to Dutch oven. Add enough broth to cover shanks by ½ inch. Bring broth to simmering.

5 Cover Dutch oven tightly and transfer to oven. Braise shanks about 1½ hours or until tender, turning 2 to 3 times. Using tongs, transfer shanks to a platter and keep warm.

6 Pour pan liquids through a fine-mesh sieve. Discard any solids and return strained liquids to the Dutch oven. Bring to boiling; reduce heat. Simmer, uncovered, about 10 minutes or until sauce thickens slightly.

7 To serve, divide Orzo Risotto among serving bowls. Top each with a veal shank and sauce; garnish each with a sprinkling of Gremolata. **Makes 4 servings**

Nutrition facts per serving: 818 cal., 40 g total fat (15 g sat. fat), 216 mg chol., 1,605 mg sodium, 52 g carb., 4 g dietary fiber, 6 g sugar, 55 g protein.

Orzo Risotto: In a large saucepan melt 6 tablespoons butter. Add ⅓ cup minced shallots and ½ teaspoon minced garlic; cook and stir over medium heat for 5 minutes or until shallots are tender. Add 1 cup orzo; cook and stir for 5 minutes or until orzo is golden. Add 3 cups boiling water and ¾ teaspoon salt. Simmer, uncovered, about 15 minutes or until orzo is tender, liquid is absorbed, and mixture is creamy. Remove from heat. Stir in 2 teaspoons finely chopped fresh thyme and 3 tablespoons chopped fresh flat-leaf parsley.

Gremolata: In a small bowl combine ⅓ cup chopped fresh flat-leaf parsley, 2 teaspoons minced garlic, 2 teaspoons lemon zest, and, if desired, 2 finely chopped anchovy fillets. Toss well to mix.

Pasta with Bolognese Sauce

PREP: 35 MINUTES   **COOK:** 15 MINUTES

- 1 pound dried pasta, such as spaghetti, linguine, or penne
- 1 pound ground veal, pork, beef, and/or turkey
- 1 cup chopped carrots (2 medium)
- ½ cup chopped onion (1 medium)
- ½ cup chopped celery (1 stalk)
- 3 cups sliced mushrooms (8 ounces)
- 6 cloves garlic, minced (1 tablespoon)
- 1 28-ounce can crushed tomatoes in puree, undrained
- 1 15-ounce can tomato sauce
- ¾ cup dry white wine
- ½ teaspoon salt
- ½ teaspoon dried rosemary, crushed
- ½ teaspoon crushed red pepper
- ¼ teaspoon ground black pepper
- ⅛ teaspoon fennel seeds, crushed
- ½ cup whipping cream

  Grated Romano or Parmesan cheese

  Fresh rosemary sprigs (optional)

1 Cook pasta according to package directions; drain. Set aside.

2 Meanwhile, in a 4- to 5-quart Dutch oven cook ground meat, carrots, onion, and celery over medium heat until meat is brown. Add mushrooms and garlic; cook for 3 to 5 minutes or until mushrooms are tender, stirring occasionally. If necessary, drain off fat.

3 Stir in tomatoes, tomato sauce, wine, salt, rosemary, red pepper, black pepper, and fennel seeds. Bring to boiling; reduce heat. Simmer, covered, for 15 minutes, stirring occasionally Stir in whipping cream; heat through. Serve sauce over hot cooked pasta. Sprinkle with grated Romano cheese. If desired, garnish with rosemary sprigs. **Makes 8 servings**

Nutrition facts per serving: 458 cal., 12 g total fat (6 g sat. fat), 74 mg chol., 734 mg sodium, 56 g carb., 4 g dietary fiber, 9 g sugar, 24 g protein.

Basque Chicken Stew

START TO FINISH: 30 MINUTES

1¼ pounds boneless, skinless chicken thighs, cut into 2-inch pieces

¼ teaspoon salt

¼ teaspoon ground black pepper

1 tablespoon olive oil

1 medium onion, thinly sliced

1 medium red sweet pepper, cut into ¼-inch-thick strips

2 cloves garlic, minced

1 14.5 ounce can diced tomatoes, drained

1 cup chicken broth

¾ pound red potatoes, cut into ½-inch wedges

½ teaspoon dried savory, crushed

1 teaspoon fresh snipped thyme, or ¼ teaspoon dried thyme, crushed

¼ teaspoon salt

⅓ cup small pimiento-stuffed green olives (optional)

Fresh thyme sprigs

1 Season chicken with salt and black pepper. In large Dutch oven heat oil over medium-high heat. Add chicken; cook about 2 minutes on side or until light brown.

2 Add onion and sweet pepper; cook about 3 minutes or until crisp-tender. Add garlic; cook for 30 seconds. Add tomatoes, broth, potatoes, savory, 1 teaspoon thyme, and salt. Bring to boiling; reduce heat. Simmer, covered, about 20 minutes or until chicken and potatoes are tender. Remove from heat. Stir in olives (if using) and garnish with additional fresh thyme. **Makes 6 servings**

Nutrition facts per serving: 320 cal., 10 g total fat (2 g sat. fat), 118 mg chol., 717 mg sodium, 25 g carb., 3 g fiber, 32 g protein.

Bowl Bit The Basques are a unique culture of people who live in the territory on the border of France and Spain. Their language is traceable to no known language, and their cuisine borrows from both countries in which they reside. This hearty stew features the favorite Basque ingredients of tomatoes, sweet peppers, and olives.

Chicken Paprikash

PREP: 15 MINUTES   **COOK:** 45 MINUTES

4 bone-in chicken breast halves
or 8 bone-in chicken thighs
(about 2 pounds total), skinned

½ teaspoon Hungarian paprika

½ teaspoon garlic powder

½ teaspoon seasoned salt

2 tablespoons olive oil

2 cups vegetable juice

2 tablespoons snipped fresh parsley

1 tablespoon Hungarian paprika

Few dashes bottled hot pepper sauce

1 8-ounce carton sour cream

½ teaspoon ground black pepper

Hot cooked spaetzle or noodles

1 Sprinkle chicken with ½ teaspoon paprika, garlic powder, and seasoned salt. In a large skillet heat oil over medium-high heat. Add chicken; cook about 10 minutes or until brown, turning to brown evenly. Add vegetable juice; stir in parsley and 1 tablespoon paprika. Bring to boiling; reduce heat. Simmer, covered, for 30 to 35 minutes or until an instant-read thermometer inserted into meat registers 170°F for breasts or 180°F for thighs.

2 Remove chicken. Cover with foil and keep warm. Remove skillet from heat. In a small bowl stir hot pepper sauce and sour cream. Gradually whisk 1 cup of the hot vegetable juice mixture into sour cream mixture. Return to mixture in skillet. Stir in black pepper. Add cooked chicken to sauce; heat through (do not boil). Serve with spaetzle or noodles. **Makes 4 servings**

Nutrition facts per serving: 579 cal., 23 g total fat (9 g sat. fat), 145 mg chol., 1,094 mg sodium, 46 g carb., 6 g dietary fiber, 45 g protein.

Bowl Bit The versions of this traditional Hungarian dish are too numerous to count, but there are two elements that appear in every one: sour cream and Hungarian paprika. Hungarians were introduced to paprika by the Turks, who ruled Hungary from 1526 to 1699. Although initially only peasants cooked with paprika, it eventually replaced black pepper. The reddish brown spice with the warm, rich flavor became so beloved by Hungarians, that they now make a distinction among eight different types, which range from a mild and bright red variety to the hottest variety, which is a light orange-brown.

Paella

1 pound fresh or frozen large shrimp in shells

8 ounces Italian sausage links, sliced

12 ounces skinless, boneless chicken breast halves, cut into ¾-inch pieces

¾ cup chopped green sweet pepper (1 medium)

⅓ cup chopped onion (1 small)

1 tablespoon finely chopped garlic

3 cups chicken broth

1½ cups long grain rice

⅛ teaspoon thread saffron, crushed

1 cup thawed frozen peas

1 cup thawed frozen cut green beans

1 Thaw shrimp, if frozen. Peel and devein shrimp; set aside.

2 In a 4-quart Dutch oven cook sausage over medium-high heat until brown. Remove sausage; set aside. Add chicken, sweet pepper, onion, and garlic to drippings in Dutch oven; cook about 10 minutes or until chicken is brown. Return sausage to Dutch oven.

3 Add broth, rice, and saffron to Dutch oven. Bring to boiling; reduce heat. Simmer, covered, for 20 minutes.

4 Stir shrimp, peas, and beans into Dutch oven; cook, covered, about 5 minutes or until shrimp turn opaque. **Makes 5 or 6 servings**

Nutrition facts per serving: 524 cal., 17 g total fat (6 g sat. fat), 74 mg chol., 1,043 mg sodium, 55 g carb., 3 g dietary fiber, 36 g protein.

Osso Buco Chicken

PREP: 30 MINUTES   BAKE: 40 MINUTES   OVEN: 350°F

¼ **cup all-purpose flour**

8 **chicken thighs, skinned**

2 **tablespoons vegetable oil**

2 **medium carrots, sliced (1 cup)**

1 **medium onion, chopped (½ cup)**

1 **stalk celery, chopped (½ cup)**

1 **clove garlic, minced**

1 **14.5-ounce can diced tomatoes, undrained**

1 **cup chicken broth**

2 **tablespoons red wine vinegar**

¼ **teaspoon dried thyme, crushed**

¼ **teaspoon ground black pepper**

1 **bay leaf**

1 **recipe Orange Gremolata**

1 Preheat oven to 350°F. Place flour in a large resealable plastic bag. Add chicken, shaking to coat.

2 In a 5- to 6-quart ovenproof Dutch oven heat oil over medium-high heat. Add chicken; cook about 4 minutes each side or until light brown. Transfer chicken to a platter. Add carrots, onion, and celery to Dutch oven; cook and stir until vegetables are brown. Add garlic; cook for 1 minute more.

3 Stir in tomatoes, broth, vinegar, thyme, pepper, and bay leaf. Return chicken to pot. Bring to boiling; cover. Transfer to oven. Cook about 40 minutes or until chicken is done and vegetables are tender, carefully removing lid and stirring halfway through. Remove and discard bay leaf before serving. Serve with Orange Gremolata. **Makes 4 servings**

Nutrition facts per serving: 320 cal., 14 g total fat (2 g sat. fat), 115 mg chol., 632 mg sodium, 18 g carb., 4 g dietary fiber, 6 g sugar, 30 g protein.

Orange Gremolata: In a small bowl combine 2 tablespoons finely chopped fresh parsley, 1 tablespoon minced garlic, 1 teaspoon finely shredded orange zest, 1 teaspoon vegetable oil, and a pinch each of salt and ground black pepper.

Coq au Vin

PREP: 40 MINUTES   **BAKE:** 45 MINUTES   **OVEN:** 350°F

2½ to 3 pounds chicken drumsticks and/or thighs, skin removed

2 tablespoons vegetable oil

Salt and ground black pepper

2 tablespoons butter

3 tablespoons all-purpose flour

1¼ cups Pinot Noir or Burgundy wine

¼ cup chicken broth or water

1 cup whole mushrooms

1 cup very thinly sliced carrots (2 medium)

⅔ cup thawed frozen small whole onions (18)

1½ teaspoons snipped fresh marjoram, or ½ teaspoon dried marjoram, crushed

1½ teaspoons snipped fresh thyme, or ½ teaspoon dried thyme, crushed

2 cloves garlic, minced

2 slices bacon, crisp-cooked, drained, and crumbled

Snipped fresh parsley (optional)

3 cups hot cooked noodles (optional)

1 Preheat oven to 350°F. In an extra-large skillet cook chicken, half at a time, in hot oil over medium heat for 10 to 15 minutes or until brown, turning occasionally. Transfer chicken to a 3-quart rectangular baking dish. Sprinkle chicken with salt and pepper. Set aside.

2 In the same skillet heat butter over medium heat until melted. Stir in flour until smooth. Gradually stir in wine and broth; cook and stir until mixture comes to boiling. Cut any large mushrooms in half. Stir mushrooms, carrots, onions, marjoram, thyme, and garlic into wine mixture. Return just to boiling. Pour vegetable mixture over chicken.

3 Bake, covered, about 45 minutes or until chicken is no longer pink (180°F). Transfer chicken and vegetable mixture to a serving platter. Top with bacon. If desired, sprinkle with parsley and serve with hot cooked noodles. **Makes 6 servings**

Nutrition facts per serving: 286 cal., 13 g total fat (4 g sat. fat), 95 mg chol., 321 mg sodium, 8 g carb., 1 g dietary fiber, 2 g sugar, 24 g protein.

Bouillabaisse

PREP: 40 MINUTES   **COOK:** 35 MINUTES   **OVEN:** BROIL 10 MINUTES

1 **pound fresh or frozen fish fillets, such as snapper, redfish, drum, mahi mahi, or grouper, cut into ½-inch pieces**

16 **large shrimp, peeled and deveined (about 8 ounces)**

¼ **cup olive oil**

2 **medium onions, chopped**

1 **medium fennel bulb, chopped**

3 **leeks (white part only), split lengthwise and chopped**

1 **tablespoon minced garlic**

4 **cups fish stock or clam juice**

2 **cups chopped tomatoes (2 large)**

4 **teaspoons finely shredded orange zest**

⅔ **cup orange juice**

2 **tablespoons chopped fresh thyme**

2 **tablespoons anise-flavored liqueur (optional)**

1 **teaspoon saffron threads**

½ **teaspoon salt**

¼ **teaspoon ground black pepper**

1½ **pounds mussels in shells, cleaned***

1 **pound oysters or scallops, shucked**

8 **1-inch-thick slices baguette-style French bread, toasted**

1 **recipe Rouille**

1 Thaw fish and/or shrimp, if frozen. Rinse fish and shrimp; pat dry with paper towels. Set aside.

2 For stock, in a large pot heat 3 tablespoons of the oil over medium heat. Add onions, fennel, leeks, and garlic; cover and cook for 10 to 12 minutes or until softened, stirring occasionally. Add stock, tomatoes, orange zest, orange juice, thyme, liqueur (if using), saffron, salt, and pepper. Bring mixture to boiling; reduce heat. Simmer, covered, for 20 minutes.

3 Meanwhile, heat remaining oil in a Dutch oven over medium-high heat. Add fish fillets; cook for 2 to 3 minutes, or until fish just flakes when tested with a fork. Add stock, mussels, oysters, and shrimp. Bring to boiling; reduce heat to medium. Cook, covered, for 3 to 5 minutes or until mussels open (discard any mussels that do not open). Divide bouillabaisse among large serving bowls. Top each with a slice of toasted baguette and about a tablespoon of Rouille. **Makes 8 servings**

Nutrition facts per serving: 400 cal., 24 g total fat (4 g sat. fat), 90 mg chol., 810 mg sodium, 22 g carb., 2 g dietary fiber, 25 g protein.

Rouille: Preheat broiler. Line broiler pan with foil. Cut ½ inch from the top and bottom of a red sweet pepper and cut lengthwise in half. Remove seeds and membranes. Broil pepper 4 to 5 inches from heat, skin side up, about 10 minutes or until skin is evenly charred. Remove from heat, carefully fold foil around the pepper, and set aside for 10 minutes. Remove pepper from foil, peel off, and discard the skin. Coarsely chop pepper; place in a blender or food processor. Add 1 tablespoon lemon juice, 2 teaspoons red wine vinegar, 1 teaspoon minced garlic, ½ teaspoon Asian chili sauce, ½ teaspoon crushed red pepper, and ½ teaspoon salt. Cover and blend or process until smooth. With machine running, add ½ cup olive oil through the opening in the lid in a slow, steady stream until combined.

***Note:** To clean live mussels, scrub under cold running water. Remove beards. For 24 mussels, in an 8-quart Dutch oven combine 4 quarts cold water and ⅓ cup salt; add mussels. Soak for 15 minutes; drain and rinse. Discard water. Repeat soaking, draining, and rinsing twice.*

Bowl Bit This Provençal fish stew originated in the French port city of Marseille, where the star ingredients are pulled from the Mediterranean Sea in abundance. The story goes that hungry fishermen, at the end of the day, cooked up the bonier and less desirable of the catch in cauldrons of sea water set over a wood fire, seasoned with garlic and fennel. Tomatoes were added sometime in the seventeenth century. Julia Child, who lived in Marseille for a year, wrote in *My Life in France* that "the telling flavor of a bouillabaisse comes from two things: the Provençal soup base—garlic, onions, tomatoes, olive oil, fennel, saffron, thyme, bay, and usually a bit of dried orange zest—and, of course, the fish—lean (non-oily), firm-fleshed, soft-fleshed, gelatinous, and shellfish." It takes a bit of time and fussing, but it is a truly impressive and gorgeous dish to make for an appreciative crowd.

Provençal Seafood Stew

START TO FINISH: 30 MINUTES

4 **jumbo shrimp (about 4 ounces)**

8 **ounces cod fillet (or other firm-fleshed fish), cut into 4 pieces**

12 **mussels in shells (about 8 ounces), cleaned***

½ **cup thinly sliced onion**

1 **clove garlic, minced**

⅛ **teaspoon ground allspice**

2 **teaspoons olive oil**

1 **14.5-ounce can peeled whole tomatoes in puree**

1 **8-ounce bottle clam juice**

¼ **teaspoon salt**

¼ **teaspoon ground black pepper**

⅛ **teaspoon crushed red pepper**

1 **teaspoon snipped fresh thyme**

½ **teaspoon finely shredded orange zest**

Fresh thyme sprigs (optional)

1 Peel and devein shrimp. Rinse shrimp, cod, and mussels; pat dry with paper towels. Set aside.

2 In a large saucepan cook onion, garlic, and allspice in hot oil over medium-high heat about 5 minutes or until onions are softened.

3 Meanwhile, press tomatoes and their juices through a fine-mesh sieve. Discard pulp and seeds. Add tomato mixture, clam juice, salt, black pepper, and crushed red pepper to the saucepan. Bring to boiling; reduce heat. Simmer, covered, for 10 minutes.

4 Stir in snipped thyme and orange zest. Add mussels, shrimp, and cod to saucepan. Gently stir to combine. Return to boiling; reduce heat. Simmer, covered, for 3 minutes more or until mussel shells open, shrimp are opaque, and fish flakes easily when tested with a fork. Discard any mussels that do not open.

5 Serve in shallow bowls and, if desired, garnish with fresh thyme sprigs. **Makes 4 servings**

Nutrition facts per serving: 145 cal., 4 g total fat, 66 mg chol., 425 mg sodium, 8 g carb., 0 g dietary fiber, 19 g protein.

*Note: *To clean live mussels, scrub mussels under cold running water. Remove beards. For 12 mussels, in a 4-quart Dutch oven combine 2 quarts cold water and 3 tablespoons salt; add mussels. Soak for 15 minutes; drain and rinse. Discard water. Repeat soaking, draining, and rinsing twice.*

Gnocchi with Creamy Tomato Sauce

PREP: 15 MINUTES   **COOK:** 8 MINUTES

- 2 17.5-ounce packages shelf-stable potato gnocchi
- 1 tablespoon olive oil
- 3 cups sliced white mushrooms
- ½ teaspoon salt
- ½ teaspoon ground black pepper
- 1¼ cups no-salt-added tomato sauce
- 1¼ cups thawed frozen peas
- 1 teaspoon dried basil
- ½ cup ricotta cheese

1 Cook gnocchi according to package directions; drain. Transfer gnocchi to a medium bowl; cover and keep warm.

2 Meanwhile, in a large nonstick skillet heat oil over medium-high heat. Add mushrooms. Sprinkle with ¼ teaspoon of the salt and ¼ teaspoon of the pepper; cook for 3 minutes.

3 Add tomato sauce, peas, and basil; reduce heat to medium. Cook for 5 minutes. Stir in ricotta cheese and the remaining salt and pepper; pour over gnocchi. Stir to combine. **Makes 6 servings**

Nutrition facts per serving: 365 cal., 6 g total fat (2 g sat. fat), 11 mg chol., 825 mg sodium, 69 g carb., 5 g dietary fiber, 10 g protein.

Gnocchi with Mushroom Sauce

PREP: 30 MINUTES   **COOK:** 16 MINUTES

2 ounces dried porcini mushrooms
  Boiling water

⅓ cup thinly sliced leek (1 medium)

3 cloves garlic, minced

2 tablespoons butter

2 tablespoons olive oil

1½ pounds portobello* and/or button
  mushrooms, sliced

1 pound cremini mushrooms, sliced

¾ cup Chardonnay or other dry white
  wine

¾ teaspoon salt

¼ teaspoon ground black pepper

⅔ cup whipping cream

2 tablespoons all-purpose flour

1 tablespoon snipped fresh
  flat-leaf parsley

2 16- or 17-ounce packages
  shelf-stable potato gnocchi

1 Soak dried mushrooms in enough boiling water to cover about 15 minutes or until soft. Drain mushrooms; discard liquid. Squeeze mushrooms to remove additional liquid.

2 Meanwhile, for mushroom sauce, in a 4- to 5-quart Dutch oven cook and stir leek and garlic in hot butter over medium heat for 2 minutes. Using a slotted spoon, remove leek mixture. Add oil to Dutch oven; heat over medium-high heat. Add all mushrooms; cook about 15 minutes or until mushrooms are lightly brown and liquid is evaporated, stirring occasionally. Stir in wine, salt, and pepper.

3 In a small bowl whisk together cream and flour; stir into mushroom mixture. Cook and stir until thickened and bubbly. Cook and stir for 1 minute more. Stir in leek mixture and parsley.

4 Meanwhile, cook gnocchi according to package directions; drain. Serve gnocchi topped with mushroom sauce. **Makes 6 servings**

Nutrition facts per serving: 543 cal., 20 g total fat (10 g sat. fat), 47 mg chol., 878 mg sodium, 78 g carb., 7 g dietary fiber, 4 g sugar, 13 g protein.

Note: *For a lighter colored sauce, use a knife or a teaspoon to gently scrape away the gills (the black portions underneath the caps) from the portobello mushrooms before slicing.*

Aglio e Olio

START TO FINISH: 15 MINUTES

- ¼ **cup olive oil**
- 4 **cloves garlic, minced**
- ½ **teaspoon crushed red pepper**
- 3 **cups steamed asparagus pieces, broccoli florets, or cauliflower florets,* and/or 8 ounces dried spaghetti, linguine, fettuccine, or mafalda pasta, cooked and drained**
- ¼ **cup finely shredded Pecorino Romano cheese (1 ounce)**
- 2 **tablespoons snipped fresh flat-leaf parsley**
- ¼ **teaspoon ground black pepper**
- **Salt**

1 In a small saucepan heat olive oil over medium heat. Add garlic and crushed red pepper; cook about 1 minute or until fragrant. Remove from heat.

2 Add garlic mixture to vegetables and/or pasta; toss gently to coat. Add cheese, parsley, and black pepper; toss gently to combine. Season to taste with salt. **Makes 6 servings**

Nutrition facts per serving: 116 cal., 10 g total fat (2 g sat. fat), 3 mg chol., 102 mg sodium, 5 g carb., 2 g dietary fiber, 3 g protein.

*Note: *To steam vegetables, place a steamer basket in a saucepan. Add water to just below the bottom of the basket. Bring water to boiling. Add vegetables to the steamer basket. Cover and reduce heat. Steam until the vegetables are crisp-tender. For asparagus, allow 3 to 5 minutes; for cauliflower or broccoli, allow 8 to 10 minutes.*

Bowl Bit The name of this simplest of Italian pasta dishes translates to "garlic and oil." Add to that a little bit of salt, black pepper, crushed red pepper, Pecorino Romano cheese, and chopped fresh parsley, and you've got a simple and very satisfying dish. Spaghetti *aglio e olio*, which originated not far from Rome in the region of Abruzzo, is associated with the rural home-style cooking known as *cucina rustica*.

Fettuccine Alfredo

START TO FINISH: 35 MINUTES

8 ounces dried fettuccine

2 tablespoons butter

1 cup whipping cream

½ teaspoon salt

⅛ teaspoon ground black pepper

½ cup freshly grated Parmesan cheese

Freshly grated Parmesan cheese (optional)

Snipped fresh parsley (optional)

1 Cook fettuccine according to package directions; drain. Set aside.

2 Meanwhile, in a large saucepan melt butter. Add whipping cream, salt, and pepper. Bring to boiling; reduce heat. Boil gently, uncovered, for 3 to 5 minutes or until mixture begins to thicken. Remove from heat. Stir in the ½ cup cheese. Add pasta to hot sauce. Toss to combine. Transfer to warm serving dish. Serve immediately. If desired, sprinkle with additional cheese and parsley. **Makes 4 servings**

Nutrition facts per serving: 515 cal., 32 g total fat (19 g sat. fat), 107 mg chol., 512 mg sodium, 45 g carb., 1 g dietary fiber, 1 g sugar, 12 g protein.

Chicken and Tomato Fettuccine Alfredo: Prepare as directed, except stir 1½ cups chopped cooked chicken (about 8 ounces) and ¼ cup drained oil-packed snipped dried tomatoes into cream mixture before adding the Parmesan cheese; heat through. Remove from heat. Stir in the ½ cup Parmesan cheese. Continue as directed.

Shrimp Fettuccine Alfredo: Prepare as directed, except stir 12 ounces cooked medium shrimp and 1 tablespoon snipped fresh basil, crushed, or 1 teaspoon dried basil into cream mixture before adding the Parmesan cheese; heat through. Remove from heat. Stir in the ½ cup Parmesan cheese. Continue as directed.

Bowl Bit This ultra rich dish has become so ubiquitous on American restaurant menus, it might seem logical that it was created in this country. It was, however, dreamed up by a Roman restaurateur named Alfredo di Lelio in 1914, as a variation on *fettuccine al burro*, or fettuccine with butter. He tweaked the dish slightly to get his pregnant wife—who was having trouble keeping food down—to eat. Though to this day the Italian version simply contains butter and cheese, the American version of this dish has come to (usually) contain cream.

Artichoke Risotto

START TO FINISH: 35 MINUTES

¼ cup chopped onion

2 teaspoons olive oil

⅓ cup arborio rice

1 clove garlic, minced

1 cup chopped kale or Swiss chard

1 14-ounce can vegetable broth

¼ cup finely shredded Romano cheese (1 ounce)

⅛ teaspoon ground black pepper

1 6-ounce jar quartered marinated artichoke hearts, drained and cut into large pieces

1 In a medium saucepan cook onion in hot oil over medium heat for 3 to 4 minutes or just until tender, stirring occasionally. Add rice and garlic; cook and stir about 2 minutes or until rice begins to brown. Add kale; cook and stir for 1 minute.

2 Meanwhile, in a small saucepan bring broth to boiling; reduce heat and simmer. Slowly add ½ cup of the broth to the rice mixture, stirring constantly. Continue to cook and stir over medium heat until liquid is absorbed. Add another ¼ cup of the broth to the rice mixture, stirring constantly. Continue to cook and stir until the liquid is absorbed. Add remaining broth, ¼ cup at a time, stirring constantly until the broth has been absorbed. (This should take about 15 minutes.)

3 Stir in cheese and pepper until cheese is melted. Stir in artichokes; heat through. **Makes 2 servings**

Nutrition facts per serving: 384 cal., 21 g total fat (5 g sat. fat), 10 mg chol., 1,205 mg sodium, 38 g carb., 1 g dietary fiber, 22 g sugar, 7 g protein.

Risotto with Beans and Vegetables

START TO FINISH: 30 MINUTES

- 3 **cups vegetable broth**
- 2 **cups sliced mushrooms**
- ½ **cup chopped onion (1 medium)**
- 2 **cloves garlic, minced**
- 2 **tablespoons olive oil**
- 1 **cup arborio rice**
- 1 **cup finely chopped zucchini (1 small)**
- 1 **cup finely chopped carrots (2 medium)**
- 1 **15-ounce can cannellini (white kidney) or pinto beans, rinsed and drained**
- ½ **cup finely shredded Parmesan cheese (2 ounces)**
- 2 **tablespoons snipped fresh flat-leaf parsley**

  Finely shredded Parmesan cheese (optional)

1 In a medium saucepan bring broth to boiling; reduce heat and simmer until needed. Meanwhile, in a large saucepan cook mushrooms, onion, and garlic in hot oil over medium heat about 5 minutes or until onion is tender. Add rice; cook and stir about 5 minutes more or until rice is golden brown.

2 Slowly add 1 cup of the broth to rice mixture, stirring constantly. Continue to cook and stir until liquid is absorbed. Add another ½ cup of the broth, the zucchini, and carrots to rice mixture, stirring constantly. Continue to cook and stir until liquid is absorbed. Add another 1 cup broth, ½ cup at a time, stirring constantly until broth is absorbed. (This should take about 20 minutes.)

3 Stir the remaining ½ cup broth into rice mixture. Cook and stir until rice is slightly creamy and just tender. Stir in beans and the ½ cup cheese; heat through. Sprinkle with parsley and, if desired, additional cheese. **Makes 4 servings**

Nutrition facts per serving: 340 cal., 11 g total fat (3 g sat. fat), 9 mg chol., 1,074 mg sodium, 53 g carb., 7 g dietary fiber, 15 g protein.

Classic Risotto with Spring Peas

START TO FINISH: 35 MINUTES

2   tablespoons olive oil

½   cup chopped onion (1 medium)

2   cloves garlic, minced

1   cup arborio rice

2   14-ounce cans vegetable broth or chicken broth

1   cup loose-pack frozen tiny or regular-size peas

¼   cup coarsely shredded carrot

2   cups fresh spinach, shredded

¼   cup grated Parmesan cheese (1 ounce)

1   tablespoon snipped fresh thyme

1 In a large saucepan heat oil over medium heat. Add onion and garlic; cook until onion is tender. Add rice; cook and stir about 5 minutes or until rice is golden brown.

2 Meanwhile, in a medium saucepan bring broth to boiling; reduce heat and simmer. Carefully add 1 cup of the broth to the rice mixture, stirring constantly. Continue to cook and stir over medium heat until liquid is absorbed. Add another 1 cup of the broth to the rice mixture, stirring constantly. Continue to cook and stir until liquid is absorbed. Add another 1 cup broth, ½ cup at a time, stirring constantly until the broth has been absorbed. (This should take 18 to 20 minutes total.)

3 Stir in remaining broth, the peas, and carrot. Cook and stir until rice is slightly firm (al dente) and creamy.

4 Stir in spinach, cheese, and thyme; heat through. Serve immediately. Makes 4 to 6 servings

Nutrition facts per serving: 252 cal., 8 g total fat (2 g sat. fat), 4 mg chol., 912 mg sodium, 38 g carb., 2 g dietary fiber, 7 g protein.

Shortcut Risotto with Spring Peas: In a medium saucepan heat olive oil over medium heat. Add onion and garlic; cook until onion is tender. Add uncooked rice; cook and stir for 2 minutes. Carefully stir in the broth. Bring to boiling; reduce heat. Cover and simmer for 20 minutes (do not lift cover). Remove from heat. Stir in peas and carrot. Cover and let stand for 5 minutes. Rice should be just tender and the mixture should be slightly creamy. (If necessary, stir in a little water to reach desired consistency.) Stir in spinach, Parmesan cheese, and thyme; heat through. Serve immediately.

Kitchen Tip Using the right rice is crucial to making a creamy, toothsome risotto. Arborio rice is the most common of the types of risotto rice. The starch content of its short, fat grains helps to create the creamy texture of a perfect risotto. Other types of risotto rice that are fairly widely available include carnaroli and vialone nano.

Kitchen Tip If desired, stir in 1 cup of chopped, cooked chicken after rice is slightly creamy and just tender; heat through.

Red Wine Risotto with Porcini Mushrooms

PREP: 20 MINUTES   COOK: 15 MINUTES   STAND: 10 MINUTES

2 14-ounce cans reduced-sodium chicken broth

1 ounce dried porcini mushrooms

¼ cup water

2 fresh thyme sprigs

1 fresh rosemary sprig

½ cup finely chopped shallots (4 medium)

2 cloves garlic, minced

2 tablespoons olive oil

1 cup arborio rice

⅓ cup dry red wine

1 tablespoon balsamic vinegar

⅛ teaspoon ground black pepper

½ cup finely shredded Pecorino Romano cheese (2 ounces)

   Fresh rosemary sprigs

1 In a medium microwave-safe bowl microwave about ¾ cup of the broth on 100 percent power (high) for 2 minutes. Add dried mushrooms. Let stand for 10 minutes.

2 Meanwhile, in a small saucepan bring the remaining broth, the water, thyme sprigs, and 1 rosemary sprig to boiling; reduce heat and simmer. Drain mushrooms, adding liquid to broth mixture in saucepan. Coarsely chop mushrooms.

3 In a large saucepan cook shallots and garlic in hot oil over medium heat until shallots are tender. Add rice; cook and stir for 1 minute. Stir in wine, vinegar, and pepper. Cook and stir until rice starts to absorb liquid. Stir in mushrooms.

4 Remove and discard herbs from broth. Slowly add 1 cup of the broth to rice mixture, stirring constantly. Continue to cook and stir over medium heat until liquid is absorbed. Add an additional ½ cup of the broth to rice mixture, stirring constantly. Continue to cook and stir until liquid is absorbed. Add the remaining broth, ½ cup at a time, stirring constantly until liquid is absorbed. (This should take 15 to 20 minutes.)

5 Top each serving with cheese and garnish with an additional rosemary sprig. **Makes 4 servings**

Nutrition facts per serving: 282 cal., 10 g total fat (3 g sat. fat), 10 mg chol., 597 mg sodium, 38 g carb., 1 g dietary fiber, 2 g sugar, 9 g protein.

Spaetzle with Caramelized Onions

START TO FINISH: 30 MINUTES

- 2 **large onions, cut into thin wedges (2 cups)**
- 2 **tablespoons butter**
- 1 **yellow, orange, and/or red sweet pepper, cut into bite-size strips**
- 4 **teaspoons packed brown sugar**
- 1 **tablespoon cider vinegar**
- ⅓ **cup chicken broth**
- ⅓ **cup half-and-half or light cream**
- 1 **tablespoon snipped fresh dill**
- ⅛ **teaspoon ground black pepper**
- 4 **ounces dried spaetzle or kluski-style egg noodles**
- 2 **cups halved Brussels sprouts**

1 In a large covered skillet cook onion in hot butter over medium-low heat for 13 to 15 minutes or until onion is tender. Add sweet pepper, brown sugar, and vinegar; cook and stir, uncovered, over medium-high heat for 4 to 5 minutes or until onion is golden. Stir in broth, half-and-half, dill, and black pepper. Boil mixture gently until thickened.

2 Meanwhile, cook spaetzle according to package directions, adding Brussels sprouts to the water with the spaetzle; drain. Return spaetzle mixture to pan. Add caramelized onion mixture to spaetzle mixture; cook and stir over low heat until spaetzle are well coated and mixture is heated through. **Makes 4 servings**

Nutrition facts per serving: 374 cal., 15 g total fat (7 g sat. fat), 106 mg chol., 279 mg sodium, 42 g carb., 5 g dietary fiber, 20 g protein.

Kitchen Tip Part dumpling, part noodle, spaetzle are tiny pillows of egg and flour that are popular in Germany, Austria, and Switzerland. Look for them in the pasta aisle of your supermarket. The curly egg noodles called kluski are of Eastern European origin. Their chewy texture and rich taste make them a delicious choice for soups and casseroles. Or try them buttered, seasoned with salt and pepper, and sprinkled with parsley for a quick side dish.

Mushroom Stroganoff

START TO FINISH: 30 MINUTES

8 ounces dried fettuccine

1 8-ounce carton sour cream

2 tablespoons all-purpose flour

¼ teaspoon salt

¼ teaspoon ground black pepper

¾ cup vegetable broth

12 ounces assorted mushrooms (such as shiitake, cremini, and/or white mushrooms)

2 medium onions, cut into thin wedges

1 clove garlic, minced

2 tablespoons butter

2 tablespoons snipped fresh parsley

1 In a large saucepan cook pasta according to package directions; drain. Return to saucepan.

2 Meanwhile, in a bowl stir together sour cream, flour, salt, and pepper. Gradually stir in the broth; set aside.

3 Remove stems from shiitake mushrooms, if using. Slice mushrooms (you should have about 4½ cups).

4 In a large skillet cook and stir mushrooms, onions, and garlic in hot butter over medium-high for 4 to 5 minutes or until tender. Add sour cream mixture to skillet; cook and stir until thickened and bubbly. Cook and stir for 1 minute more.

5 Pour mushroom mixture over hot cooked pasta; toss gently to coat. Transfer to a serving platter; sprinkle with parsley. **Makes 4 servings**

Nutrition facts per serving: 439 cal., 21 g total fat (12 g sat. fat), 41 mg chol., 419 mg sodium, 54 g carb., 3 g dietary fiber, 5 g sugar, 13 g protein.

Make-It-Mine European Bowl

PREP: 35 MINUTES   COOK: 20 MINUTES

3 pounds sausage, page 118

3 pounds potatoes

   Vinaigrette, page 118

   Toppers, page 119

   Garnishes, page 119

Basic Instructions

1 Prick sausages in several places with a fork. Place sausages in a Dutch oven or large pot, add cold water to cover. Bring to boiling; reduce heat. Simmer, covered, for 20 minutes. Remove Dutch oven from heat; keep sausages warm in the hot water.

2 Place potatoes in another Dutch oven or large pot. Add cold water to cover. Bring to boiling; reduce heat. Simmer, covered, for 15 to 20 minutes or until potatoes are just tender. Drain potatoes. If desired, quarter potatoes while still warm. Transfer potatoes to a warm, large shallow bowl.

3 In a jar with a screw-top lid combine Vinaigrette ingredients. Shake jar vigorously to blend. Pour vinaigrette over warm potatoes. Toss gently to coat, taking care not to break the potatoes.

4 Slice warm sausages into 2-inch lengths. To serve, divide warm potatoes among warmed serving bowls. Top with sausage pieces, sprinkle with Toppers. Garnish as desired. **Makes 8 servings**

SAUSAGE

French

French garlic sausage

Spanish

Mild Spanish chorizo

German

Bockwurst, knockwurst, or bratwurst

Italian

Mild Italian sausage

Greek

Chicken sausage with spinach and feta cheese or with spinach and Asiago cheese

Irish

Bangers or mild, unsmoked pork and beef sausage

VINAIGRETTE

French

⅔ cup extra-virgin olive oil

¼ cup dry white wine

¼ cup red wine vinegar

2 tablespoons reduced-sodium chicken broth

1 tablespoon coarse-grain Dijon mustard

½ teaspoon salt

¼ teaspoon ground black pepper

Spanish

⅔ cup extra-virgin olive oil

¼ cup dry white wine

5 tablespoons sherry vinegar

2 teaspoons whole grain mustard

½ teaspoon salt

¼ teaspoon ground black pepper

¼ teaspoon smoked paprika

German

⅔ cup extra-virgin olive oil

5 tablespoons malt vinegar

¼ cup light lager beer

2 teaspoons mustard seeds

½ teaspoon dry mustard

½ teaspoon salt

¼ teaspoon ground black pepper

Italian

⅔ cup extra-virgin olive oil

5 tablespoons white balsamic vinegar

¼ cup dry white wine

¼ cup chopped fresh basil

2 cloves garlic, minced

½ teaspoon salt

¼ teaspoon ground black pepper

Greek

⅔ cup extra-virgin olive oil

¼ cup dry white wine

3 tablespoons lemon juice

2 tablespoons orange juice

2 tablespoons minced fresh oregano

2 cloves minced garlic

½ teaspoon salt

¼ teaspoon crushed fennel seeds

¼ teaspoon ground black pepper

Irish

⅓ cup cider vinegar

¼ cup dry sherry

2 tablespoons chicken broth

1 tablespoon spicy brown mustard

½ teaspoon salt

¼ teaspoon ground black pepper

TOPPERS

French

¼ cup crumbled blue cheese

2 tablespoons chopped fresh chives

Spanish

Shaved Manchego cheese

Chives

Chopped fresh cilantro (1 tablespoon)

German

Coarsely grated Gouda cheese

Italian

Shaved Pecorino Romano cheese

Greek

Crumbled feta cheese

Irish

Small cubes of Dubliner cheese

GARNISHES

French

2 tablespoons chopped fresh flat-leaf parsley

Cornichons or small sour pickles (optional)

Artichoke hearts (optional)

Spanish

1 tablespoon chopped fresh chives

1 tablespoon chopped fresh cilantro

Spanish green olives (optional)

½ cup chopped Marcona almonds (optional)

German

2 tablespoons chopped fresh chives

2 tablespoons fresh parsley

Room-temperature refrigerated sauerkraut (optional)

Chopped hard-boiled eggs (optional)

Italian

2 tablespoons chopped fresh parsley

Sliced roasted red sweet peppers (optional)

Pitted kalamata olives (optional)

Fresh basil leaves (optional)

Greek

2 tablespoons chopped fresh parsley

Pitted kalamata olives (optional)

Finely sliced red onion (optional)

Blanched asparagus spears (optional)

Irish

2 tablespoons chopped fresh parsley

Cored and thinly sliced apple (optional)

Thinly sliced red onion (optional)

The American bowl

Beef and Noodles

PREP: 30 MINUTES   COOK: 1 HOUR 40 MINUTES

- 1 pound boneless beef round steak or chuck roast
- ¼ cup all-purpose flour
- 1 tablespoon vegetable oil
- ½ cup chopped onion (1 medium)
- 2 cloves garlic, minced
- 3 cups beef broth
- 1 teaspoon dried marjoram or basil, crushed
- ¼ teaspoon ground black pepper
- 8 ounces frozen egg noodles
- 2 tablespoons snipped fresh parsley

1 Trim fat from meat. Cut meat into ¾-inch cubes. Place flour in a resealable plastic bag. Add meat cubes, a few at a time, shaking to coat. In a large saucepan heat oil over medium-high heat. Add half of the meat; cook until brown. Remove meat from saucepan. Add the remaining meat, the onion, and garlic to the saucepan; cook until meat is brown (if necessary, add more oil). Drain off fat. Return all meat to the saucepan.

2 Stir in broth, marjoram, and pepper. Bring to boiling; reduce heat. Simmer, covered, for 1¼ to 1½ hours or until meat is tender.

3 Stir noodles into broth mixture. Bring to boiling; reduce heat. Cook, uncovered, for 25 to 30 minutes or until noodles are tender. Sprinkle servings with parsley. **Makes 4 servings**

Nutrition facts per serving: 351 cal., 12 g total fat (3 g sat. fat), 94 mg chol., 677 mg sodium, 29 g carb., 1 g dietary fiber, 2 g sugar, 31 g protein.

Beef Ragout with Gravy

PREP: 45 MINUTES   **COOK:** 1 HOUR 50 MINUTES

¼ cup all-purpose flour

2 pounds boneless beef chuck roast, cut into 1-inch cubes

3 tablespoons vegetable oil

4 cups water

½ cup chopped onion (1 medium)

1 clove garlic, minced

2 bay leaves

2 teaspoons Worcestershire sauce

1 teaspoon sugar

1 teaspoon lemon juice

½ teaspoon salt

½ teaspoon ground black pepper

½ teaspoon paprika

Pinch ground allspice

6 tiny new potatoes, halved

6 medium carrots, quartered

1 pound boiling onions, peeled

2 tablespoons water

1 tablespoon all-purpose flour

¼ cup dry sherry (optional)

Snipped fresh parsley

1 Place ¼ cup flour in a resealable plastic bag. Add meat cubes, a few at a time, shaking to coat. In a 4-quart Dutch oven heat oil over medium-high heat. Add beef cubes, one-third at a time; cook and stir until beef is brown. Drain off fat. Return all beef to Dutch oven. Add the 4 cups water, chopped onion, garlic, and bay leaves. Stir in Worcestershire sauce, sugar, lemon juice, salt, pepper, paprika, and allspice. Bring to boiling; reduce heat. Simmer, covered, for 1½ to 2 hours or until meat is nearly tender.

2 Add potatoes, carrots, and boiling onions. Return to boiling; reduce heat. Simmer, covered, for 20 to 30 minutes more or until vegetables are tender. Remove bay leaves; discard. Using a slotted spoon, transfer meat and vegetables to a serving dish. Cover and keep warm.

3 For gravy, in a small bowl combine 2 tablespoons water and 1 tablespoon flour; stir into liquid in Dutch oven; cook and stir until thickened and bubbly. Cook and stir for 1 minute more. If desired, stir in sherry. Pour gravy over meat and vegetables. Sprinkle with parsley. **Makes 6 to 8 servings**

Nutrition facts per serving: 320 cal., 8 g total fat (2 g sat. fat), 89 mg chol., 348 mg sodium, 26 g carb., 4 g dietary fiber, 35 g protein.

Bowl Bit A ragout is a hearty, saucy, well-seasoned stew of meat and vegetables. The spelling is the English version of the French word *ragoût*—which is the same kind of stew, only (of course) French. Italian *ragù* is a thick, meaty sauce for pasta.

Bistro Beef Steak with Wild Mushroom Ragout

START TO FINISH: 35 MINUTES

3 cloves garlic, minced

2 teaspoons herbes de Provence

½ teaspoon ground black pepper

¼ teaspoon salt

3 8-ounce boneless beef top loin steaks, cut ¾ inch thick

1 tablespoon olive oil

⅓ cup finely chopped shallots

2 cloves garlic, minced

8 ounces assorted wild mushrooms (oyster, cremini, and/or shiitake), sliced*

¼ cup dry sherry (optional)

1 14-ounce can reduced-sodium beef broth

1 tablespoon cornstarch

1 Preheat broiler. In a small bowl combine 3 minced garlic cloves, 1 teaspoon of the herbes de Provence, the pepper, and salt. Trim fat from beef steaks. Sprinkle herb mixture over all sides of the steaks; rub in with your fingers. Place steaks on the unheated rack of broiler pan. Broil 3 to 4 inches from the heat for 9 to 11 minutes for medium-rare to medium doneness (145°F to 160°F), turning once.

2 Meanwhile, for mushroom ragout, in a large nonstick skillet heat oil over medium-high heat. Add shallots and 2 minced garlic cloves; cook for 1 to 3 minutes or until shallots are tender. Add mushrooms; cook for 6 to 7 minutes or until mushrooms are tender and any liquid evaporates, stirring occasionally. Remove from heat. Stir in sherry (if using). Return to heat; bring to boiling. Cook, uncovered, for 30 to 60 seconds or until liquid evaporates.

3 In a medium bowl stir together beef broth, cornstarch, and the remaining herbes de Provence. Stir broth mixture into mushroom mixture; cook and stir over medium heat until thickened and bubbly. Cook and stir for 2 minutes more.

4 Cut each steak in half and serve topped with the mushroom ragout. **Makes 6 servings**

Nutrition facts per serving: 206 cal., 8 g total fat (2 g sat. fat), 66 mg chol., 291 mg sodium, 4 g carb., 1 g dietary fiber, 27 g protein.

*Note: *Stem the oyster and shiitake mushrooms before slicing.*

Kitchen Tip Herbes de Provence is a blend of dried herbs that grow in profusion in the south of France. It usually contains basil, fennel seed, lavender, marjoram, rosemary, sage, savory, and thyme.

Chipotle-Braised Short Ribs and Cheesy Polenta

PREP: 50 MINUTES   **COOK:** 3 HOURS

3 pounds boneless beef short ribs, or 12 bone-in beef short ribs

1 teaspoon kosher salt, or ¾ teaspoon salt

½ teaspoon ground black pepper

⅓ cup all-purpose flour

1 tablespoon vegetable oil

2 cups dry red wine or cranberry juice

1 14-ounce can beef broth, or 1¾ cups beef stock

1 tablespoon snipped fresh thyme, or 1 teaspoon dried thyme, crushed

3 cloves garlic, peeled

1 bay leaf

2 tablespoons sugar

8 ounces carrots, cut into chunks

2 small parsnips, peeled and sliced

1 10-ounce package red pearl onions, peeled* (15 to 20)

1 cup chopped, seeded tomato (1 large)

1 to 2 chipotle chile peppers in adobo sauce, drained and chopped

1 recipe Cheesy Polenta

Snipped fresh thyme (optional)

1 Trim fat from meat. Sprinkle meat with salt and pepper. Place flour in a shallow dish. Dip meat in flour, coating well on all sides. In a 6- to 8-quart Dutch oven cook meat, half at a time, in hot oil over medium-high heat until brown. Add wine, broth, dried thyme (if using), garlic, and bay leaf. Bring to boiling; reduce heat. Simmer, covered, for 2 hours.

2 Meanwhile, in a large saucepan bring lightly salted water to boiling. Add sugar; stir until sugar is dissolved. Add carrots, parsnips, and onions; cook, uncovered, for 5 to 7 minutes or until vegetables are tender. Drain. Submerge vegetables in a large bowl of ice water. Let stand for 5 minutes to cool quickly. Drain; cover and chill until ready to use.

3 Add tomato, 1 tablespoon fresh thyme (if using), and chipotle peppers to meat mixture. Simmer, covered, for 30 minutes. Add chilled vegetables. Return to boiling. Simmer, covered, for 30 minutes more or until meat is very tender. Remove bay leaf; discard.

4 To serve, using a slotted spoon, remove beef and vegetables; arrange in shallow bowls. Spoon Cheesy Polenta alongside beef and vegetable mixture. Skim fat from cooking juices; spoon some of the juices over meat and vegetables in bowls. If desired, garnish with snipped fresh thyme. **Makes 6 servings**

Nutrition facts per serving: 463 cal., 15 g total fat (6 g sat. fat), 60 mg chol., 1,100 mg sodium, 43 g carb., 5 g dietary fiber, 11 g sugar, 25 g protein.

Cheesy Polenta:
In a large saucepan bring 2½ cups water to boiling. Meanwhile, in a medium bowl combine 1 cup yellow cornmeal, 1 cup cold water, and ½ teaspoon salt. Slowly add cornmeal mixture to boiling water, stirring constantly. Cook and stir until mixture returns to boiling. Reduce heat to low. Cook, uncovered, for 10 to 15 minutes or until mixture is very thick, stirring occasionally. Before serving, stir in ¼ cup milk. Gently stir in ½ cup finely shredded Parmesan cheese (2 ounces) until melted.

***Note:** To peel onions easily, blanch onions in boiling water for 30 seconds. Drain and cool. Cut a thin slice off each root end and squeeze from the other end to remove each peel.*

Cincinnati Chili

PREP: 30 MINUTES   **COOK:** 45 MINUTES

5   bay leaves

1   teaspoon whole allspice

2   pounds lean ground beef

2   cups chopped onions (2 large)

1   clove garlic, minced

2   tablespoons chili powder

1   teaspoon ground cinnamon

¼   to ½ teaspoon cayenne pepper

4   cups water

1   15-ounce can red kidney beans, rinsed and drained

1   8-ounce can tomato sauce

1   tablespoon vinegar

1   teaspoon Worcestershire sauce

½   teaspoon salt

¼   teaspoon ground black pepper

   Hot cooked spaghetti

   Shredded cheddar cheese (optional)

1 For a spice bag, cut a 6- to 8-inch square from a double thickness of 100-percent-cotton cheesecloth. Place bay leaves and allspice in center of the cheesecloth square. Bring up the corners; tie closed with kitchen string. Set aside.

2 In a 4-quart Dutch oven cook meat, onions, and garlic over medium-high heat until meat is brown and onion is tender, stirring to break up meat as it cooks. Drain off fat. Stir in chili powder, cinnamon, and cayenne pepper; cook and stir for 1 minute.

3 Stir in the water, beans, tomato sauce, vinegar, Worcestershire sauce, salt, and black pepper. Add spice bag. Bring to boiling; reduce heat. Simmer, covered, for 30 minutes. Simmer, uncovered, for 15 to 20 minutes more or until desired consistency, stirring occasionally. Remove spice bag; discard. Serve chili over hot cooked spaghetti. If desired, top with cheese. **Makes 8 servings**

Nutrition facts per serving : 257 cal., 11 g total fat (4 g sat. fat), 71 mg chol., 435 mg sodium, 16 g carb., 5 g dietary fiber, 25 g protein.

Bowl Bit So why do Cincinnatians like their chili infused with sweet spices such as cinnamon, cloves, and allspice—and served on top of spaghetti? The story goes that in the early 1920s, a couple of immigrant restaurateurs from Macedonia wanted to expand their menus beyond their own ethnic cuisine. The result was this regional specialty. They began serving it at their hot dog stand, next to a burlesque theater called the Empress, and soon followed up by opening a "chili parlor" by the same name—the first of the city's many chili parlors. Today, according to the Greater Cincinnati Convention and Visitor's Bureau, Cincinnatians eat more than 2 million pounds of chili a year.

Goulash

PREP: 25 MINUTES   **COOK:** 1 HOUR 15 MINUTES

- 2 tablespoons vegetable oil
- 1 pound beef top round steak, cut into ½-inch cubes
- ½ cup chopped onion (1 medium)
- 2 tablespoons all-purpose flour
- 1 tablespoon Hungarian paprika
- 2 cloves garlic, minced
- 3 14-ounce cans chicken broth
- 1 14.5-ounce can diced tomatoes, undrained
- 1½ cups sliced carrots (3 medium)
- 2 tablespoons tomato paste
- 1 bay leaf
- ½ teaspoon dried marjoram, crushed
- ½ teaspoon caraway seeds, crushed
- ½ teaspoon ground black pepper
- 2 cups peeled and cubed potatoes
- Sour cream (optional)

1 In a 4- to 5-quart Dutch oven heat oil over medium-high heat. Add meat and onion; cook about 5 minutes or until meat is brown and onion is tender.

2 Add flour, paprika, and garlic; cook for 3 minutes, stirring constantly. Stir in broth, tomatoes, carrots, tomato paste, bay leaf, marjoram, caraway seeds, and pepper. Bring to boiling; reduce heat. Simmer, covered, for 50 minutes, stirring occasionally. Add potatoes; simmer, covered, for 25 to 30 minutes more or until potatoes and beef are tender. Remove bay leaf; discard. If desired, top each serving with sour cream. **Makes 6 to 8 servings**

Nutrition facts per serving: 244 cal., 9 g total fat (2 g sat. fat), 42 mg chol., 996 mg sodium, 19 g carb., 3 g dietary fiber, 21 g protein.

Savory Beef Stew

PREP: 25 MINUTES   **BAKE:** 2 HOURS 45 MINUTES   **OVEN:** 325°F

1   2½- to 3-pound boneless beef chuck pot roast

⅓   cup all-purpose flour

5   slices bacon

3   cups sliced mushrooms

1   medium onion, chopped (½ cup)

2   to 3 cups water

¼   cup chili sauce

2   teaspoons instant beef bouillon granules

½   teaspoon dried thyme, crushed

½   teaspoon dried basil, crushed

¼   teaspoon ground black pepper

6   medium carrots, cut into 1½-inch pieces (1 pound)

1   cup frozen peas

1 Preheat oven to 325°F. Trim fat from meat. Cut meat into 1½-inch cubes. Place flour in a resealable plastic bag. Add a few cubes of meat at a time, shaking to coat; set aside.

2 In an large Dutch oven cook bacon until crisp. Remove bacon; reserve drippings in Dutch oven. Drain bacon on paper towels. Crumble bacon; set aside. Remove all but 3 tablespoons drippings from Dutch oven; reserve remaining drippings.

3 Brown meat, half at a time, in hot drippings, adding more drippings if necessary. Remove all meat from Dutch oven. Add mushrooms and onion; cook until tender. Return meat to Dutch oven. Add bacon, 2 cups of the water, chili sauce, bouillon granules, thyme, basil, and pepper. Bring to boiling. Place Dutch oven in oven. Bake, covered, for 2½ hours. (Add more water, if necessary during cooking.)

4 Meanwhile, cook carrots in boiling water about 10 minutes or until just tender; drain. Stir carrots into stew. Sprinkle frozen peas over mixture. Bake, covered, about 15 minutes more or until meat is tender. **Makes 6 servings**

Nutrition facts per serving: 446 cal., 18 g total fat (6 g sat. fat), 97 mg chol., 819 mg sodium, 21 g carb., 4 g dietary fiber, 7 g sugar, 49 g protein.

Kitchen Tip Cooking the carrots separately for a shorter amount of time, then adding them to the stew toward the end of cooking time, keeps them brightly colored and sweet—just tender enough but not mushy.

Potato-Topped Beef Bowl

START TO FINISH: 19 MINUTES   **OVEN:** BROIL

1   pound ground beef

1   16-ounce package frozen mixed vegetables

2   cups shredded cheddar cheese (8 ounces)

¼   cup snipped fresh flat-leaf parsley

¼   teaspoon salt

⅛   teaspoon ground black pepper

2   cups boiling water

2   cups instant mashed potato flakes

2   tablespoons butter, melted

1 Preheat broiler. In an extra-large skillet brown beef over medium-high heat; drain off fat. Stir in frozen vegetables; cook, stirring occasionally, until heated through. Stir in half of the cheese, half of the parsley, the salt, and pepper.

2 Meanwhile, in large bowl combine 2 cups boiling water, potato flakes, and 1 tablespoon of the butter. Stir until smooth. Season to taste with salt and pepper; set aside.

3 Divide beef mixture among four 16-ounce broiler-safe dishes. Top with potatoes; sprinkle with the remaining cheese. Broil 3 inches from heat for 2 to 3 minutes or until cheese is melted. Drizzle with the remaining butter; sprinkle with the remaining parsley. **Makes 4 servings**

Nutrition facts per serving: 677 cal., 42 g total fat (22 g sat. fat), 152 mg chol., 693 mg sodium, 35 g carb., 5 g dietary fiber, 0 g sugar, 41 g protein.

Spaghetti and Meatballs

PREP: 35 MINUTES   **COOK:** 1 HOUR

1   cup finely chopped onion (1 large)

1   cup finely chopped carrot
    (1 medium)

½   cup finely chopped celery (1 stalk)

3   cloves garlic, minced

2   tablespoons olive oil

2   15-ounce cans tomato sauce

1   cup water

1   cup dry red wine

3   tablespoons snipped fresh Italian
    parsley

10 fresh basil leaves, torn

1   tablespoon dried Italian seasoning

1   tablespoon tomato paste

1   teaspoon sugar

½   teaspoon crushed red pepper
    (optional)

3   bay leaves

    Salt and freshly ground black pepper

1   recipe Beef-Sausage Meatballs

1   pound dried spaghetti, cooked
    and drained

    Freshly grated Parmesan cheese

1 In a 4-quart Dutch oven cook onion, carrot, celery, and garlic in hot oil about 15 minutes or until vegetables are tender, stirring occasionally.

2 Stir in tomato sauce, the water, wine, parsley, basil, Italian seasoning, tomato paste, sugar, crushed red pepper (if using), and bay leaves.

3 Bring to boiling; reduce heat. Simmer, uncovered, for 45 to 60 minutes or until desired consistency, stirring occasionally. Remove bay leaves; discard. Season to taste with salt and pepper.

4 Meanwhile, prepare Beef-Sausage Meatballs. Gently drop meatballs, one at a time, into sauce. Stir gently to coat with sauce. Cover and cook about 30 minutes or until meatballs are done.*

5 Serve sauce and meatballs over hot cooked spaghetti. Sprinkle with Parmesan cheese. **Makes 6 to 8 servings**

Nutrition facts per serving: 757 cal., 34 g total fat (11 g sat. fat), 129 mg chol., 1,681 mg sodium, 65 g carb., 4 g dietary fiber, 36 g protein.

Beef-Sausage Meatballs: In a large bowl combine ¼ cup milk; 1 lightly beaten egg; ½ cup fine dry bread crumbs; ¼ cup finely snipped fresh parsley; ¼ cup freshly grated Parmesan cheese (1 ounce); 1 teaspoon dried Italian seasoning, crushed; ½ teaspoon salt; and ¼ teaspoon ground black pepper. Add 1 pound ground beef and 12 ounces bulk Italian sausage; mix well. Form meat mixture into meatballs, each about 1½ inches in diameter. In a large skillet heat 2 tablespoons olive oil over medium heat. Add meatballs; cook about 10 minutes or until brown, turning occasionally.

*Note: *The internal color of a meatball is not a reliable doneness indicator. A beef or sausage meatball cooked to 160°F is safe, regardless of color. To measure the doneness of a meatball, insert an instant-read thermometer into the center of the meatball.*

Winter Beef Ragout

PREP: 30 MINUTES   **COOK:** 1 HOUR 30 MINUTES

2 tablespoons vegetable oil

1 pound boneless beef chuck roast, cut into ¾-inch cubes

2 14-ounce cans beef broth

2 teaspoons snipped fresh oregano, or ¾ teaspoon dried oregano, crushed

2 teaspoons snipped fresh basil, or ¾ teaspoon dried basil, crushed

2 teaspoons Worcestershire sauce

½ teaspoon ground black pepper

2 cups cubed Yukon gold potatoes or other potatoes

1 cup frozen cut green beans

1 cup sliced carrots (2 medium)

1 cup sliced celery (2 stalks)

1 15-ounce can Great Northern beans, rinsed and drained

1 14.5-ounce can diced tomatoes, undrained

1 small yellow summer squash or zucchini, sliced

Fresh basil leaves (optional)

1 In a 4-quart Dutch oven heat oil. Add beef cubes, half at a time, to hot oil; cook and stir until brown. Drain off fat. Return all beef to Dutch oven. Add broth, dried oregano and basil (if using), Worcestershire sauce, and pepper. Bring to boiling; reduce heat. Simmer, covered, for 1 hour.

2 Add potatoes, green beans, carrots, and celery. Return to boiling; reduce heat. Simmer, covered, for 20 minutes. Stir in beans, tomatoes, squash, and fresh oregano and basil (if using). Return to boiling; reduce heat. Simmer, covered, about 5 minutes more or just until squash is tender. If desired, garnish each serving with fresh basil leaves. **Makes 6 servings**

Nutrition facts per serving: 307 cal., 7 g total fat (2 g sat. fat), 36 mg chol., 552 mg sodium, 33 g carb., 6 g dietary fiber, 4 g sugar, 27 g protein.

Texas Bowl o' Red Chili

PREP: 30 MINUTES   **COOK:** 1 HOUR 30 MINUTES

3 pounds boneless beef chuck roast, cut into ½-inch cubes

1 teaspoon salt

½ teaspoon freshly ground black pepper

1 tablespoon vegetable oil

4 cups chopped onions (4 large)

3 tablespoons chili powder

3 tablespoons yellow cornmeal

6 cloves garlic, minced

1 tablespoon ground cumin

2 teaspoons dried oregano, crushed

¼ teaspoon cayenne pepper

1 14-ounce can beef broth

1¼ cups water

1 tablespoon packed brown sugar

Chopped onion (optional)

Fresh oregano (optional)

1 Sprinkle beef with ½ teaspoon of the salt and ¼ teaspoon of the black pepper. In a 4-quart Dutch oven heat oil. Add one-third of the beef; cook until brown. Using a slotted spoon, remove beef, reserving drippings in pan. Repeat with remaining beef, cooking one-third at a time (if necessary, add more oil).

2 Add 4 cups chopped onions to drippings; cook over medium-high heat about 5 minutes or until tender. Stir in chili powder, cornmeal, garlic, cumin, oregano, and cayenne pepper; cook for 30 seconds. Stir in beef, broth, water, brown sugar, and remaining salt and black pepper. Bring to boiling; reduce heat. Simmer, covered, for 1½ to 2 hours or until meat is tender. If desired, top each serving with additional chopped onion and fresh oregano. **Makes 6 servings**

Nutrition facts per serving: 448 cal., 17 g total fat (5 g sat. fat), 107 mg chol., 812 mg sodium, 19 g carb., 4 g dietary fiber, 53 g protein.

Beef, Mango, and Spiced Bulgur Bowls

START TO FINISH: 30 MINUTES

1 cup reduced-sodium chicken broth

⅔ cup bulgur

1 clove garlic, minced

½ teaspoon ground cumin

¼ teaspoon ground coriander

⅛ teaspoon ground cinnamon

⅛ teaspoon cayenne pepper

6 ounces reduced-sodium deli roast beef, cut into thin strips*

½ of a medium mango, peeled and cut up*

½ cup fresh snow peas, tips and strings removed and halved crosswise*

¼ cup sliced scallions (2)*

¼ cup snipped fresh cilantro*

¼ cup unsalted peanuts, chopped (optional)

1 In a 1½-quart microwave-safe casserole combine broth, bulgur, garlic, cumin, coriander, cinnamon, and cayenne pepper. Microwave, covered, on 100 percent power (high) about 4 minutes or until boiling. Remove from microwave. Let stand about 20 minutes or until bulgur is tender. Drain, if necessary.

2 To serve, divide bulgur mixture among serving bowls. Top with beef, mango, snow peas, scallions, cilantro, and (if desired) peanuts. **Makes 4 servings**

Nutrition facts per serving: 164 cal., 2 g total fat (1 g sat. fat), 26 mg chol., 421 mg sodium, 25 g carb., 5 g dietary fiber, 5 g sugar, 13 g protein.

*Note: *Maximize your time by cutting up the beef, mango, vegetables, and cilantro during the bulgur's standing time.*

U.S. Senate Bean Soup

STAND: OVERNIGHT   PREP: 35 MINUTES   COOK: 1 HOUR 50 MINUTES

1¼ cups dried small white beans, such as navy or Great Northern

1 meaty ham hock

2 14-ounce cans reduced-sodium chicken broth

3 cups cold water

1 large onion, chopped

3 stalks celery, chopped

4 cloves garlic, minced

½ teaspoon ground black pepper

4 cups chopped kale

1 pound medium red-skinned potatoes, quartered

⅓ cup milk

2 tablespoons butter

½ teaspoon salt

¼ cup chopped fresh parsley (optional)

1 Soak beans overnight in 8 cups cold water. Drain; rinse well. Drain again. (Or, in a large pot cover dried beans with 8 cups cold water. Bring to boiling over medium-high heat. Remove from heat and let stand 1½ hours. Drain; rinse well. Drain again.)

2 In a large pot combine beans, ham hock, broth, and the 3 cups water. Bring to boiling over medium-high heat; reduce heat to low. Simmer, covered, for 1 to 1½ hours or until beans are just tender. Transfer ham hock to a plate. When cool enough to handle, cut meat off bone; discard bone. Coarsely chop meat; add to pot.

3 Add onion, celery, garlic, and pepper to pot. Simmer, covered, for 15 minutes. Add kale; cook, uncovered, for 5 to 10 minutes more or until vegetables and beans are tender. Season to taste with salt and pepper.

4 Meanwhile, in a medium saucepan cover potatoes with water. Bring to boiling; reduce heat. Simmer, covered, for 15 minutes or until very tender. Drain potatoes; return to pan. Add milk, butter, and ½ teaspoon salt. Mash to desired consistency. Cover and keep warm.

5 To serve, place scoops of mashed potatoes in shallow soup bowls. Ladle soup over potatoes in bowls. If desired, sprinkle with parsley. **Makes 6 servings**

Nutrition facts per serving: 320 cal., 6 g total fat (3 g sat. fat), 31 mg chol., 872 mg sodium, 47 g carb., 13 g dietary fiber, 21 g protein.

Bowl Bit Every day, visitors to the U.S. Senate restaurant have the opportunity to enjoy a hearty bowl of U.S. Senate Bean Soup. Depending on which story you believe, that is thanks to Senator Knute Nelson of Minnesota, Senator Fred Dubois of Idaho, or Speaker of the House Joe Cannon. In soup as in politics, there are very different ideas about the same subject. One Senate story goes that in the early 1900s, Dubois—who chaired the committee on restaurants—introduced a resolution to require that the soup be available every day. Another says that in 1903 Nelson requested that the soup be a fixture on the menu. The House version of the story goes that Cannon arrived at the House restaurant one day in 1904 to find the soup missing from the menu— reportedly because it was a very hot and humid day and the cook decided no one would want to eat hot soup on such a day. "Thunderation," Cannon supposedly cried, "I had my mouth set for bean soup! From now on, hot or cold, rain, snow or shine, I want it on the menu every day." None of these stories has been verified by Senate historians, but it does make good folklore. Traditionally, U.S. Senate Bean Soup is thickened with potatoes. This version serves the soup—freshened up with a little kale—on top of creamy mashed potatoes.

Chili Verde

2 tablespoons vegetable oil

2 pounds lean boneless pork, cut into ¾-inch cubes

½ cup chopped onion (1 medium)

½ cup chopped green sweet pepper (1 small)

¼ cup chopped celery

2 tablespoons chopped scallion (1)

1 clove garlic, minced

2 tablespoons all-purpose flour

2¼ cups water

1 15-ounce can golden hominy, drained

1 11- to 13-ounce can tomatillos, drained and cut up

2 4.5-ounce cans diced green chiles, drained

Flour tortillas (optional)

Sour cream (optional)

Chopped tomatoes (optional)

Snipped fresh cilantro (optional)

1 In a 4-quart Dutch oven heat 1 tablespoon of the oil. Add half of the pork; cook over medium heat until brown. Using a slotted spoon, remove pork; reserve. Repeat with remaining pork, reserving drippings in pan. Add onion, sweet pepper, celery, scallion, and garlic to drippings; cook and stir about 5 minutes or until tender. Stir in the remaining 1 tablespoon oil and the flour; cook and stir for 5 minutes more.

2 Stir meat and the water into vegetable mixture. Bring to boiling. Stir in hominy, tomatillos, and green chiles. Return to boiling; reduce heat. Simmer, uncovered, about 30 minutes or until pork is tender, stirring occasionally. If desired, serve with tortillas, sour cream, tomatoes, and cilantro. **Makes 6 to 8 servings**

Nutrition facts per serving: 327 cal., 13 g total fat (3 g sat. fat), 95 mg chol., 701 mg sodium, 16 g carb., 3 g dietary fiber, 35 g protein.

Hoppin' John

PREP: 25 MINUTES   **COOK:** 25 MINUTES   **STAND:** 10 MINUTES

1   cup dried black-eyed peas

4   slices bacon, diced

1   medium onion, chopped (½ cup)

4   cups water

8   ounces ham, diced

¼   teaspoon cayenne pepper

1   teaspoon ground black pepper

¾   cup converted long-grain rice

3   scallions, chopped (⅓ cup)

1 Rinse black-eyed peas; set aside.

2 In a large Dutch oven cook bacon over medium heat for 8 minutes or until crisp. Remove bacon; reserve drippings in Dutch oven. Drain on paper towels; set aside.

3 Add onion to bacon drippings; cook about 5 minutes or until tender. Stir in black-eyed peas, the water, ham, cayenne pepper, and black pepper. Bring to boiling; reduce heat. Simmer, covered, for 20 minutes.

4 Stir in rice. Bring to boiling; reduce heat. Simmer, covered, for 15 minutes. Remove from heat. Let stand, covered, for 10 minutes. Just before serving, stir in scallions and cooked bacon. **Makes 8 servings**

Nutrition facts per serving: 226 cal., 11 g total fat (4 g sat. fat), 30 mg chol., 589 mg sodium, 19 g carb., 2 g dietary fiber, 1 g sugar, 11 g protein.

Bowl Bit The American South's version of a rice-and-bean dish eaten throughout West Africa, Hoppin' John has become required eating on New Year's Day in order to bring about a prosperous year filled with good luck. No one really knows how it got its name, but it is mentioned in a British writer's nineteenth-century travelogue, *A Journey in the Seaboard Slave States*. "The greatest luxury with which they are acquainted is a stew of bacon and peas, with red pepper," he wrote, "which they call 'Hopping John.'" A recipe for the dish also appears in an 1847 cookbook called *The Carolina Housewife*.

Jambalaya

PREP: 25 MINUTES   **COOK:** 20 MINUTES

- 1 **pound fresh or frozen peeled and deveined shrimp**
- 2 **tablespoons vegetable oil**
- ½ **cup chopped onion (1 medium)**
- ⅓ **cup chopped celery**
- ¼ **cup chopped green sweet pepper**
- 2 **cloves garlic, minced**
- 2 **cups chicken broth**
- 1 **14.5-ounce can diced tomatoes, undrained**
- 8 **ounces andouille or kielbasa sausage, halved lengthwise and cut into ½-inch slices**
- ¾ **cup long grain rice**
- 1 **teaspoon dried thyme, crushed**
- ½ **teaspoon dried basil, crushed**
- ¼ **teaspoon ground black pepper**
- ¼ **teaspoon cayenne pepper**
- 1 **bay leaf**
- 4 **ounces cooked boneless ham, cut into bite-size cubes (1 cup)**

1 Thaw shrimp, if frozen.

2 In a 12-inch skillet heat oil over medium heat. Add onion, celery, sweet pepper, and garlic; cook and stir for 5 minutes. Stir in broth, tomatoes, sausage, rice, thyme, basil, black pepper, cayenne pepper, and bay leaf. Bring to boiling; reduce heat. Simmer, covered, for 15 minutes. Stir in shrimp. Return to boiling. Simmer, covered, about 5 minutes more or until shrimp turn opaque and rice is tender. Stir in ham; heat through. Remove and discard bay leaf. **Makes 6 servings**

Nutrition facts per serving: 416 cal., 20 g total fat (6 g sat. fat), 154 mg chol., 1,199 mg sodium, 27 g carb., 1 g dietary fiber, 4 g sugar, 30 g protein.

Bowl Bit This rice-based dish that came out of New Orleans's French Quarter is essentially an American version of the Spanish dish paella. However, because the cost of importing saffron was prohibitive, tomatoes became the substitute. Although this story from *The Dictionary of American Food and Drink* is likely a fanciful fabrication, it is nonetheless fun mythology: "Late one evening a traveling gentleman stopped by a New Orleans inn which had little food remaining from the evening meal. The traveler instructed the cook, '*Jean, balayez!*' or 'Jean, sweep something together!' in the local dialect. The guest pronounced the resulting hodge-podge dish as 'Jean balayez.'"

Pork and Pumpkin Noodle Bowl

START TO FINISH: 30 MINUTES

8 ounces dried whole wheat linguine

1 small red onion, thinly sliced

1 tablespoon olive oil

1 pound pork loin, cut in ½-inch-thick slices

3 tablespoons reduced-sodium soy sauce

   Ground black pepper

12 fresh sage leaves

1 teaspoon minced garlic (2 cloves), or ½ teaspoon garlic powder

1 cup canned or frozen pureed pumpkin or butternut squash

1 cup water

¼ cup blue cheese crumbles (optional)

1 Cook pasta according to package directions, adding onion during the last 5 minutes of cooking time; drain. Keep warm.

2 Meanwhile, in a 12-inch skillet heat oil over medium heat. Brush pork with some soy sauce and generously sprinkle with pepper. Cook sage leaves in hot oil until crisp. Drain on paper towels. Add pork to skillet; cook about 2 minutes each side or until golden outside and slightly pink inside. Remove pork from skillet; cover and keep warm.

3 In same skillet combine remaining soy sauce, garlic, ¼ cup of the pumpkin, and the water. Bring to boiling; reduce sauce slightly. Add pasta and onions to skillet; heat through. Divide pasta among bowls. In skillet heat the remaining pumpkin. Serve pork with pasta, pumpkin, sage leaves, and blue cheese. **Makes 4 servings**

Nutrition facts per serving: 414 cal., 9 g total fat (2 g sat. fat), 71 mg chol., 645 mg sodium, 51 g carb., 2 g dietary fiber, 5 g sugar, 34 g protein.

Polenta-Sausage Bowl

START TO FINISH: 20 MINUTES   **OVEN:** BROIL

1 16-ounce tube refrigerated polenta with sun-dried tomatoes

2 medium zucchini, halved lengthwise

1 tablespoon vegetable oil

Salt and ground black pepper

1 pound bulk Italian sausage

1 8-ounce package sliced white mushrooms

1 cup grape tomatoes

1 teaspoon dried Italian seasoning, crushed

Finely shredded Parmesan cheese (optional)

1 Preheat broiler. Lightly grease baking sheet. Cut polenta into 12 slices. Place polenta and zucchini on baking sheet. Brush with oil; sprinkle with salt and pepper. Broil 4 to 5 inches from heat for 8 to 10 minutes or until polenta is lightly brown and zucchini is crisp-tender, turning once.

2 Meanwhile, in a large skillet cook sausage over medium heat until it begins to brown, using a wooden spoon to break up sausage as it cooks. Drain off fat. Add mushrooms, tomatoes, and Italian seasoning to skillet; cook about 5 minutes or until sausage is no longer pink. Slice zucchini crosswise. Place polenta in serving bowls and spoon sausage mixture and zucchini over polenta. Sprinkle with cheese. **Makes 4 servings**

Nutrition facts per serving: 547 cal., 40 g total fat (13 g sat. fat), 86 mg chol., 1,340 mg sodium, 26 g carb., 3 g dietary fiber, 23 g protein.

Pork and Hominy Soup

START TO FINISH: 30 MINUTES

12 ounces lean boneless pork

 1 tablespoon vegetable oil

 1 cup chopped onion (1 large)

 2 cloves garlic, minced

 4 cups chicken broth

 2 medium carrots, thinly sliced (1 cup)

¼ teaspoon ground cumin

¼ teaspoon crushed red pepper

 1 14.5-to 15- ounce can hominy, drained

 3 tablespoons snipped fresh cilantro

¼ cup shredded radishes

    Lime wedges

1 If desired, partially freeze pork for easier slicing. Thinly slice pork across the grain into bite-size strips.

2 In a large saucepan heat oil over medium heat. Add pork strips, onion, and garlic; cook and stir until brown. Remove pork mixture from saucepan; reserve. Add broth, carrots, cumin, and crushed red pepper to saucepan. Bring to boiling; reduce heat. Simmer, covered, about 8 minutes or just until carrots are tender. Return pork mixture to saucepan. Add hominy and cilantro; heat through. Top each serving with radishes. Serve with lime wedges. **Makes 4 servings**

Nutrition facts per serving: 281 cal., 10 g total fat (2 g sat. fat), 49 mg chol., 1,262 mg sodium, 24 g carb., 4 g dietary fiber, 23 g protein.

Pork and Ale Ragout

PREP: 25 MINUTES   **COOK:** 35 MINUTES

2   tablespoons all-purpose flour

½   teaspoon crushed red pepper

1   pound boneless pork sirloin, cut into ¾-inch cubes

1   tablespoon vegetable oil

2   cloves garlic, minced

3   cups vegetable broth

1   12-ounce can beer, or 1½ cups vegetable broth

3   medium parsnips, peeled and cut into ¾-inch slices

2   large sweet potatoes, peeled and cut into 1-inch cubes

1   medium onion, cut into thin wedges

2   tablespoons snipped fresh thyme, or 1½ teaspoons dried thyme, crushed

1   tablespoon packed brown sugar

1   tablespoon Dijon mustard

4   large tomatoes, coarsely chopped

2   small Granny Smith apples, cored and cut into wedges

1 Combine flour and red pepper in a resealable plastic bag. Add pork cubes, a few at a time, shaking to coat.

2 In a 4-quart Dutch oven heat oil over medium heat. Add half of pork and garlic to hot oil; cook and stir until pork is brown. Remove from pot. Repeat with remaining pork and garlic. Return all pork mixture to pot. Add broth, beer, parsnips, sweet potatoes, onion, thyme, brown sugar, and mustard.

3 Bring to boiling; reduce heat. Simmer, covered, for 30 minutes. Stir in tomatoes and apples. Return to boiling; reduce heat. Simmer, covered, about 5 minutes more or until meat, vegetables, and apples are tender. **Makes 6 servings**

Nutrition facts per serving: 288 cal., 7 g total fat (2 g sat. fat), 48 mg chol., 571 mg sodium, 36 g carb., 6 g dietary fiber, 9 g sugar, 20 g protein.

Red Beans and Rice

PREP: 25 MINUTES   **COOK:** 2 HOURS

1 pound dried red kidney beans or dried red beans (about 2½ cups)

2 tablespoons butter

½ cup chopped onion (1 medium)

1 to 2 cloves garlic, minced

1 tablespoon all-purpose flour

1 pound cooked andouille or kielbasa sausage, halved lengthwise and cut into ½-inch slices

1 meaty smoked ham shank or pork hock

1 teaspoon ground black pepper

6 cups water

½ teaspoon salt

5 cups hot cooked white or brown rice

Corn bread (optional)

1 Rinse beans. In a large pot combine beans and 8 cups water. Cover and let soak in a cool place for 8 hours or overnight. (Or bring beans and 8 cups water to boiling; reduce heat. Simmer, uncovered, for 2 minutes. Remove from heat. Cover and let stand for 1 hour.) Drain beans. Rinse; set aside. Wipe pot dry.

2 In the same pot melt butter over medium heat. Add onion and garlic; cook and stir until onion is tender but not brown. Sprinkle flour over onion mixture; stir to combine. Carefully stir in beans, sausage, ham shank, pepper, and 6 cups fresh water. Bring to boiling; reduce heat. Simmer, covered, for 1½ to 2 hours or until beans are tender, stirring occasionally.

3 Remove ham shank. When cool enough to handle, cut meat off bone; discard bone. Coarsely chop meat; return to pot. Return to boiling; reduce heat. Simmer, uncovered, about 20 minutes more or until heated through and a thick gravy forms, stirring occasionally. Season with salt. Serve bean mixture over hot cooked rice. If desired, serve with corn bread. **Makes 10 servings**

Nutrition facts per serving: 470 cal., 18 g total fat (7 g sat. fat), 41 mg chol., 908 mg sodium, 53 g carb., 7 g dietary fiber, 24 g protein.

Bowl Bit This humble Louisiana Creole dish was traditionally made on Mondays with beans and the leftover pork bones and/or sausage from Sunday dinner. Monday was usually laundry day—a good day for a long-simmering dish. The unwatched pot could bubble away while women were busy scrubbing clothes.

Sausage and Vegetable Ragout

START TO FINISH: 35 MINUTES

1 **8-ounce package cooked chicken andouille sausage links or cooked smoked turkey sausage links, cut into ½-inch-thick slices**

1 **medium yellow crookneck squash, cut into ½-inch pieces**

1 **14-ounce can reduced-sodium chicken broth**

1 **tablespoon snipped fresh rosemary, or 1 teaspoon dried rosemary, crushed**

2 **cups coarsely chopped fresh escarole, Swiss chard, baby kale, and/or spinach leaves**

1 **15-ounce can white kidney beans (cannellini beans), rinsed and drained**

1 **cup carrots cut into thin, bite-size sticks**

Ground black pepper

Purchased garlic croutons (optional)

In a large saucepan combine sausage, squash, broth, and rosemary. Bring to boiling; reduce heat. Simmer, uncovered, for 5 minutes. Stir in escarole, beans, and carrots. Return to boiling; reduce heat. Simmer, covered, about 5 minutes more or until vegetables are tender. Season to taste with pepper. If desired, top each serving with croutons. **Makes 4 servings**

Nutrition facts per serving: 156 cal., 8 g total fat (2 g sat. fat), 20 mg chol., 785 mg sodium, 20 g carb., 7 g dietary fiber, 16 g protein.

Chicken and Dumplings

PREP: 30 MINUTES   COOK: 47 MINUTES

2½ to 3 pounds meaty chicken
   pieces (breast halves, thighs,
   and drumsticks)

3 cups water

1 medium onion, cut into wedges

¾ teaspoon salt

½ teaspoon dried sage or marjoram,
   crushed

¼ teaspoon black pepper

1 bay leaf

1 cup sliced celery (2 stalks)

1 cup thinly sliced carrots (2 medium)

1 cup sliced mushrooms

1 recipe Dumplings

½ cup cold water

¼ cup all-purpose flour

1 Skin chicken. In a 4-quart Dutch oven combine chicken, the 3 cups water, onion, salt, sage, pepper, and bay leaf. Bring to boiling; reduce heat. Simmer, covered, for 25 minutes. Add celery, carrots, and mushrooms. Return to boiling; reduce heat. Simmer, covered, about 10 minutes more or until vegetables are tender and chicken is no longer pink (170°F for breasts, 180°F for thighs and drumsticks). Remove and discard bay leaf. Using tongs, rearrange the chicken pieces so they rest on top of the vegetables.

2 Meanwhile, prepare Dumplings. Spoon dumpling batter into 6 mounds on top of the chicken. (Do not spoon batter into the liquid.) Return to boiling; reduce heat. Simmer, covered, for 12 to 15 minutes or until a wooden toothpick inserted into a dumpling comes out clean. Do not lift cover while simmering. Using a slotted spoon transfer chicken, dumplings, and vegetables to a serving platter; keep warm.

3 For gravy, pour cooking liquid into a large measuring cup. Skim fat from liquid; discard fat. Measure 2 cups cooking liquid, adding broth if necessary. Pour liquid back into Dutch oven. Combine the ½ cup cold water and flour. Stir mixture into liquid in Dutch oven. Cook and stir over medium heat until mixture is thickened and bubbly. Cook and stir for 1 minute more. Serve gravy over chicken, vegetables, and dumplings. **Makes 6 servings**

Nutrition facts per serving: 322 cal., 11 g total fat (3 g sat. fat), 77 mg chol., 672 mg sodium, 25 g carb., 2 g dietary fiber, 4 g sugar, 29 g protein.

Dumplings: In a medium bowl combine 1 cup all-purpose flour, 1 teaspoon baking powder, and ½ teaspoon salt. Cut in 2 tablespoons shortening until mixture resembles coarse crumbs. Add ½ cup buttermilk, stirring just until moistened.

Spicy Chicken Chili

STAND: 1 HOUR **PREP:** 30 MINUTES **COOK:** 2 HOURS

1 **pound dried Great Northern beans (2½ cups)**

1 **tablespoon vegetable oil**

2 **cups chopped onions (2 large)**

2 **4.5-ounce cans diced green chiles**

4 **cloves garlic, minced**

2 **teaspoons ground cumin**

1½ **teaspoons dried oregano, crushed**

¼ **teaspoon ground cloves**

¼ **teaspoon cayenne pepper**

4 **14-ounce cans chicken broth**

4 **cups coarsely chopped cooked chicken***

1 **12-ounce can beer**

1 **cup shredded Monterey Jack cheese or Monterey Jack cheese with jalapeño chile peppers (4 ounces)**

Sour cream (optional)

Bottled salsa (optional)

Snipped fresh cilantro (optional)

Shredded Monterey Jack cheese (optional)

1 Rinse beans. In a large pot combine beans and enough water to cover. Bring to boiling; reduce heat. Simmer, uncovered, for 2 minutes. Remove from heat. Cover and let stand for 1 hour. (Or place beans in water in pot. Cover and let soak in a cool place for 6 to 8 hours or overnight.) Drain beans. Rinse; set aside.

2 In same large pot heat oil over medium heat. Add onions; cook for 5 to 8 minutes or until tender. Stir in green chiles, garlic, cumin, oregano, cloves, and cayenne pepper; cook and stir for 2 minutes more. Stir in beans and broth. Bring to boiling; reduce heat. Simmer, covered, about 2 hours or until beans are very tender.

3 Stir in chicken, beer, and 1 cup cheese; cook and stir until cheese is melted. If desired, serve with sour cream, salsa, cilantro, and/or additional cheese. **Makes 12 servings**

Nutrition facts per serving: 306 cal., 7 g total fat (3 g sat. fat), 52 mg chol., 834 mg sodium, 29 g carb., 9 g dietary fiber, 30 g protein.

***Note:** For cooked chicken, place 2 pounds boneless, skinless chicken breast halves in a large skillet or saucepan; add enough water to cover. Bring to boiling; reduce heat. Simmer, covered, for 15 to 20 minutes or until chicken is tender and no longer pink. Drain; cool slightly. Coarsely chop chicken.*

Tex-Mex Chicken Stew

PREP: 25 MINUTES   **COOK:** 20 MINUTES

- 2 **tablespoons butter**
- 1 **pound skinless, boneless chicken breast halves, cut into bite-size pieces**
- 1 **large sweet potato, peeled and sliced**
- ½ **cup chopped onion (1 medium)**
- 1 **to 2 fresh serrano chile peppers, halved and seeded***
- ½ **teaspoon ground coriander**
- ¼ **teaspoon ground cumin**
- 3 **cups chicken broth**
- 1 **15.5-ounce can golden hominy, rinsed and drained, or 1 cup thawed frozen whole kernel corn**
- **Sour cream (optional)**
- **Thinly sliced fresh serrano chile peppers* (optional)**

1 In a large saucepan or Dutch oven melt butter. Add chicken, half at a time; cook and stir until no longer pink. Using a slotted spoon, remove chicken, reserving drippings in saucepan.

2 Add sweet potato, onion, chile pepper, coriander, and cumin to saucepan. Add 1½ cups of the broth. Bring to boiling; reduce heat. Simmer, covered, about 20 minutes or until vegetables are very tender. Cool slightly.

3 Transfer sweet potato mixture to a blender. Cover and blend until smooth. Return to saucepan. Stir in chicken, the remaining 1½ cups broth, and hominy; heat through. If desired, top each serving with sour cream and/or thinly sliced chile peppers. **Makes 4 to 6 servings**

Nutrition facts per serving: 330 cal., 9 g total fat (4 g sat. fat), 84 mg chol., 1,080 mg sodium, 29 g carb., 5 g dietary fiber, 31 g protein.

***Note:** Because chile peppers contain volatile oils that can burn your skin and eyes, avoid direct contact with them as much as possible. When working with chile peppers, wear plastic gloves. If your bare hands touch the chile peppers, wash your hands well with soap and water.*

Chicken and Sausage Gumbo

PREP: 45 MINUTES   **COOK:** 1 HOUR 2 MINUTES

1 cup all-purpose flour

⅔ cup vegetable oil

1 cup sliced celery (2 stalks)

1 cup chopped green sweet pepper (1 large)

½ cup chopped onion (1 medium)

2 cloves garlic, minced

8 ounces cooked smoked sausage, cut into 1-inch pieces

8 ounces andouille sausage, cut into ½-inch pieces

2 pounds meaty chicken pieces, skinned if desired (breast halves, thighs, and drumsticks)

5 cups water

1 teaspoon salt

¼ to ½ teaspoon cayenne pepper

¼ teaspoon ground black pepper

Hot cooked rice (optional)

1 For roux, in a large heavy Dutch oven stir together flour and oil until smooth. Cook over medium-high heat for 5 minutes. Reduce heat to medium. Cook and stir for 10 to 15 minutes or until roux is reddish brown in color (the deeper the color, the richer and more flavorful the gumbo). Stir in celery, sweet pepper, onion, and garlic; cook for 5 minutes more, stirring occasionally. Add sausages; cook until sausages are light brown.

2 Add chicken, the water, salt, cayenne pepper, and black pepper. Bring to boiling; reduce heat. Simmer, covered, about 1 hour or until chicken is tender and no longer pink (170°F for breasts; 180°F for thighs and drumsticks).

3 Skim off fat. Remove chicken from Dutch oven; cool slightly. When chicken is cool enough to handle, remove meat from bones; discard bones. Coarsely chop chicken; return to Dutch oven. Cook for 2 to 3 minutes or until chicken is heated through. If desired, serve with rice. **Makes 10 servings**

Nutrition facts per serving: 460 cal., 34 g total fat (9 g sat. fat), 72 mg chol., 961 mg sodium, 12 g carb., 1 g dietary fiber, 25 g protein.

Bowl Bit Originating in southern Louisiana in the eighteenth century, gumbo is truly a mélange of culinary influences. The French, Spanish, Germans, West Africans, and Choctaw Indians all threw something in the pot. There are two main varieties of gumbo—Creole and Cajun. Creole gumbo usually contains shellfish and tomatoes. Cajun gumbo is generally darker in color, spicier, and based on shellfish and poultry. Gumbo is further distinguished by the type of thickener used—African okra, the Choctaw spice filé powder (the ground root of the sassafras tree), or French roux. The word *gumbo* is likely derived from the African word for *okra* (*ki ngombo*) or the Choctaw word for *filé* (*kombo*).

Sweet Potato–Corn Chowder

PREP: 30 MINUTES   **COOK:** 35 MINUTES

12 ounces andouille, kielbasa, or smoked pork sausage, halved lengthwise and cut into ½-inch slices

1 cup chopped onion (1 large)

1 cup chopped celery (2 stalks)

1 tablespoon minced garlic (6 cloves)

3 tablespoons all-purpose flour

1½ teaspoons ground cumin

1½ teaspoons chili powder

1 teaspoon Cajun or Creole seasoning

6 cups chicken broth

1 16-ounce package thawed frozen whole kernel corn, or 3 cups fresh sweet corn kernels

2 cups ½-inch cubes peeled sweet potatoes (about 2 small)

12 ounces skinless, boneless chicken breast halves, cut into ¾-inch pieces

1 cup whipping cream

1 teaspoon ground black pepper

1 In a 6-quart Dutch oven brown sausage over medium heat for 5 minutes, stirring occasionally. Add onion, celery, and garlic; cook and stir for 5 minutes. Stir in flour, cumin, chili powder, and Cajun seasoning; cook and stir for 2 minutes more. Stir in chicken broth. Bring to boiling.

2 Add corn, sweet potatoes, and chicken. Return to boiling; reduce heat. Simmer, covered, about 20 minutes or until sweet potatoes are tender. Stir in whipping cream and pepper; heat through. **Makes 8 to 10 servings**

Nutrition facts per serving: 408 cal., 25 g total fat (13 g sat. fat), 86 mg chol., 1,161 mg sodium, 27 g carb., 3 g dietary fiber, 6 g sugar, 19 g protein.

Hearty Chicken and Noodles

PREP: 45 MINUTES   **COOK:** 35 MINUTES

3 chicken legs (thigh-drumstick portions; about 2 pounds total)

2¼ cups water

1 14-ounce can reduced-sodium chicken broth

1 bay leaf

1 tablespoon snipped fresh thyme, or 1 teaspoon dried thyme, crushed

¾ teaspoon salt

¼ teaspoon ground black pepper

2 cups sliced carrots (4 medium)

1½ cups chopped onions (2 large)

3 cups dried wide noodles

2 cups milk

2 tablespoons all-purpose flour

1 cup thawed frozen peas

1 Skin chicken. In a 4- to 5-quart Dutch oven combine chicken, the water, broth, bay leaf, dried thyme (if using), salt, and pepper. Add carrots and onions. Bring to boiling; reduce heat. Simmer, covered, about 30 minutes or until chicken is no longer pink (180°F). Remove and discard bay leaf.

2 Remove chicken from Dutch oven; cool slightly. When chicken is cool enough to handle, remove meat from bones; discard bones. Chop or shred chicken; set aside.

3 Return vegetable mixture to boiling. Add noodles; cook, uncovered, for 5 minutes. Stir in 1½ cups of the milk.

4 In a screw-top jar, combine the remaining milk and the flour. Cover and shake until combined. Stir into noodle mixture; cook and stir over medium heat until thickened and bubbly. Stir in chicken, peas, and fresh thyme (if using); cook for 1 to 2 minutes more or until heated through. **Makes 6 servings**

Nutrition facts per serving: 316 cal., 6 g total fat (2 g sat. fat), 102 mg chol., 624 mg sodium, 37 g carb., 4 g dietary fiber, 27 g protein.

Chicken-Broccoli Mac and Cheese

START TO FINISH: 21 MINUTES

8   ounces dried rigatoni

2   cups fresh broccoli florets

1   2- to 2¼-pound deli-roasted chicken

1   5.2-ounce package semisoft cheese
    with garlic and fine herbs

¾   to 1 cup milk

¼   cup oil-pack dried tomatoes, drained
    and snipped

¼   teaspoon ground black pepper

    Snipped fresh flat-leaf parsley
    (optional)

1 Cook pasta according to package directions, adding broccoli florets during the last 3 minutes of cooking time. Drain pasta and broccoli; set aside.

2 Meanwhile, remove meat from roasted chicken. Coarsely chop chicken.

3 In same pot combine cheese, ¾ cup milk, tomatoes, and pepper; cook and stir until cheese is melted. Add pasta mixture and chicken. Heat through. If necessary, thin with additional milk. If desired, sprinkle with parsley. **Makes 4 servings**

Nutrition facts per serving: 667 cal., 34 g total fat (15 g sat. fat), 163 mg chol., 872 mg sodium, 52 g carb., 3 g dietary fiber, 6 g sugar, 40 g protein.

Three-Bean Ragout with Mushrooms and Smoked Chicken

STAND: 1 HOUR   PREP: 30 MINUTES   COOK: 1 HOUR 45 MINUTES

½ cup dried flageolet beans

½ cup dried New Mexico Red Appaloosa beans

½ cup dried South Runner beans

4 cups water

2 bay leaves

12 ounces chanterelle or shiitake mushrooms, coarsely chopped

2 stalks celery, chopped (1 cup)

2 medium carrots, chopped (1 cup)

1 small white onion, chopped (⅓ cup)

1 tablespoon butter

1 cup shredded smoked chicken or deli-roasted chicken, shredded (6 ounces)

1 tablespoon snipped fresh sage

2 cups chicken broth

Salt and ground black pepper

Fresh sage sprigs (optional)

1 Rinse beans. In a large saucepan combine beans and 5 cups of water. Bring to boiling. Remove from heat. Cover and let stand for 1 hour. (Or place beans with cold water to cover in saucepan. Cover and let soak in a cool place for 6 to 8 hours or overnight.)

2 Drain beans; rinse. Return beans to saucepan along with 4 cups fresh water and the bay leaves. Bring to boiling; reduce heat. Simmer, covered, until beans are tender, about 1½ hours. Drain beans. Remove and discard bay leaves.

3 In a large saucepan cook mushrooms, celery, carrots, and onion in hot butter for 5 to 7 minutes or until vegetables are tender. Stir in chicken, sage, broth, and beans. Bring to boiling; reduce heat. Simmer, uncovered, for 10 minutes. Season to taste with salt and pepper. Garnish with fresh sage sprigs, if desired. **Makes 4 to 6 servings**

Nutrition facts per serving: 400 cal., 10 g total fat (3 g sat. fat), 34 mg chol., 735 mg sodium, 55 g carb., 10 g dietary fiber, 26 g protein.

Kitchen Tip If you can't find the flageolet beans, New Mexico Red Appaloosa beans, and South Runner beans called for in this recipe, simply use 1½ cups of your favorite dried bean mix.

Classic Cioppino

PREP: 45 MINUTES   **COOK:** 30 MINUTES   (pictured on page 4)

8 fresh clams in shells

2 8-ounce fresh or frozen lobster tails

8 ounces fresh or frozen fish fillets (such as halibut, red snapper, perch, or sea bass)

8 ounces fresh or frozen peeled and deveined shrimp

½ cup sliced mushrooms

⅓ cup chopped green or red sweet pepper

¼ cup chopped onion

2 cloves garlic, minced

1 tablespoon olive oil

1 14.5-ounce can diced tomatoes, undrained

⅓ cup dry red wine or white wine

¼ cup water

2 tablespoons snipped fresh parsley

2 tablespoons tomato paste

1 tablespoon lemon juice

1½ teaspoons snipped fresh basil, or ½ teaspoon dried basil, crushed

1½ teaspoons snipped fresh oregano, or ½ teaspoon dried oregano, crushed

1 teaspoon sugar

¼ teaspoon salt

⅛ teaspoon crushed red pepper

1 Using a stiff brush, scrub clam shells under cold running water. In a large pot or bowl combine 8 cups water and 3 tablespoons salt. Add clams; soak for 15 minutes. Drain and rinse clams; discard water. Repeat soaking, draining, and rinsing two more times.

2 Meanwhile, thaw lobster, fish, and shrimp, if frozen. Remove and discard skin from fish, if present. Rinse lobster, fish, and shrimp; pat dry with paper towels. Cut fish into 1½-inch pieces. Cover and chill lobster, fish, and shrimp until needed.

3 In a 4- to 5-quart Dutch oven cook mushrooms, sweet pepper, onion, and garlic in hot oil until tender. Stir in tomatoes, wine, the ¼ cup water, parsley, tomato paste, lemon juice, dried basil and oregano (if using), sugar, salt, and crushed red pepper. Bring to boiling; reduce heat. Simmer, covered, for 20 minutes.

4 Add lobster and fresh basil and oregano (if using). Return to boiling; reduce heat. Simmer, covered, for 5 minutes. Add clams, fish, and shrimp. Return to boiling; reduce heat. Simmer, covered, for 5 to 10 minutes more or until clams open, fish flakes easily, and lobster and shrimp are opaque. Discard any unopened clams. **Makes 4 servings**

Nutrition facts per serving: 326 cal., 6 g total fat (1 g sat. fat), 255 mg chol., 1,181 mg sodium, 13 g carb., 3 g dietary fiber, 6 g sugar, 50 g protein.

Bowl Bit Italian fishermen in San Francisco's North Beach in the late 1800s created cioppino (chuh-PEE-noh)—a tomato and wine-based stew studded with the catch of the day. The name likely comes from the word *ciuppin*, which means "to chop" in the Ligurian dialect from the Italian port city of Genoa, a description of the process of chopping up the leftover crab, clams, shrimp, scallops, squid, mussels, and fish to make the stew.

Weekday Cioppino

START TO FINISH: 35 MINUTES

2　pounds fresh skinless salmon, cod, and/or sea scallops

2　medium fennel bulbs, trimmed and thinly sliced

3　tablespoons olive oil

4　cloves garlic, minced

3　cups coarsely chopped tomatoes (3 medium)

1　14- or 15-ounce can fish stock* or chicken broth

1　teaspoon dried oregano, crushed, or 2 teaspoons snipped fresh oregano

½　teaspoon anise seeds, crushed (optional)

　　Salt and freshly ground black pepper

　　Fennel fronds or shredded fresh basil

1 Rinse fish and/or scallops; pat dry with paper towels. If using fish, cut into 2-inch pieces. Set aside.

2 In a 4- to 6-quart Dutch oven cook sliced fennel in hot oil over medium heat about 10 minutes or until tender, stirring occasionally. Add garlic; cook and stir for 1 minute more.

3 Add tomatoes, stock, dried oregano (if using), and anise seeds (if using). Bring to boiling. Stir in fish and/or scallops.

4 Return to boiling; reduce heat. Simmer, uncovered, for 6 to 8 minutes or until fish flakes easily when tested with a fork and scallops are opaque.

5 Season to taste with salt and pepper. Stir in fresh oregano (if using). Garnish each serving with fennel fronds. **Makes 8 servings**

Nutrition facts per serving: 178 cal., 6 g total fat (1 g sat. fat), 49 mg chol., 169 mg sodium, 9 g carb., 3 g dietary fiber, 2 g sugar, 22 g protein.

*Note: *To make your own fish stock, use 1½ pounds fresh or frozen fish heads and tails or drawn lean fish (such as cod, pike, flounder, haddock, hake, orange roughy, or porgy). Thaw fish, if frozen. Rinse fish; pat dry with paper towels. Place fish in a Dutch oven. Add 4 cups water; 1 stalk celery with leaves, cut up; ½ of a medium onion, cut into wedges; 2 tablespoons lemon juice; 2 teaspoons dried marjoram, crushed; 2 teaspoons grated fresh ginger or ½ teaspoon ground ginger; 2 cloves garlic, halved; ¼ teaspoon salt; and ¼ teaspoon dry mustard. Bring to boiling; reduce heat. Simmer, covered, for 45 minutes. Strain stock; discard solids. Makes 3½ cups.*

Shrimp and Cheddar Grits

START TO FINISH: 35 MINUTES

1 pound medium shrimp in shells

4 cups water

½ teaspoon salt

1 cup stone-ground grits

1 cup shredded sharp cheddar cheese (4 ounces)

1 tablespoon butter

2 cups sliced mushrooms

1 clove garlic, minced

1 tablespoon peanut oil

⅛ teaspoon ground black pepper

   Few dashes bottled hot pepper sauce

4 slices bacon, crisp-cooked, drained, and crumbled

¼ cup sliced scallions (2)

3 tablespoons snipped fresh parsley

1 Peel and devein shrimp. Rinse shrimp; pat dry with paper towels. Cut shrimp in half lengthwise. Set aside.

2 In a large saucepan bring the water and salt to boiling. Gradually stir in grits. Reduce heat to low. Cook, uncovered, for 20 minutes or until thick, stirring frequently. Add cheese and butter, stirring until melted; set aside.

3 Meanwhile, in a large skillet cook mushrooms and garlic in hot oil over medium heat for 3 minutes. Increase heat to medium-high. Add shrimp; cook and stir for 2 to 3 minutes more or until shrimp turn opaque. Stir in pepper and hot pepper sauce until combined.

4 Transfer grits to a serving dish. Top with shrimp mixture. Sprinkle with bacon, scallions, and parsley. **Makes 6 servings**

Nutrition facts per serving: 312 cal., 14 g total fat (3 g sat. fat), 146 mg chol., 572 mg sodium, 22 g carb., 2 g dietary fiber, 25 g protein.

Shrimp Etouffee with Andouille Dirty Rice

START TO FINISH: 1 HOUR 10 MINUTES

2 pounds fresh or frozen large shrimp

2 tablespoons vegetable oil

2 tablespoons all-purpose flour

½ cup finely chopped onion (1 medium)

1 8-ounce package dirty rice mix

4 ounces cooked andouille sausage, chopped

½ cup finely chopped celery (1 stalk)

¼ cup finely chopped red sweet pepper

2 cloves garlic, minced

2¾ cups reduced-sodium chicken broth

⅓ cup butter

3 tablespoons all-purpose flour

1 cup chopped onion (1 large)

1 cup chopped yellow sweet pepper (1 large)

½ cup chopped celery (1 stalk)

2 cups water

1 bay leaf

¼ teaspoon bottled hot pepper sauce

½ cup chopped scallions (4)

1 Thaw shrimp, if frozen. Peel and devein shrimp; leave tails intact, if desired. In a large saucepan heat oil over medium-high heat. Add 2 tablespoons flour; cook and stir 3 to 4 minutes or until mixture turns nut brown.

2 Add ½ cup onion; cook and stir over low heat until onion is golden. Add dirty rice mix, sausage, finely chopped celery, red sweet pepper, and garlic; cook and stir over low heat for 4 to 5 minutes or until rice is golden. Slowly add broth. Bring mixture to boiling; reduce heat. Simmer, covered, for 25 minutes. Keep warm.

3 Meanwhile, in a large skillet melt butter over medium heat. Add 3 tablespoons flour, stirring to combine. Cook, stirring constantly, for 6 to 8 minutes, until flour mixture is light nut brown. Add 1 cup onion, yellow sweet pepper, and chopped celery; cook and stir about 5 minutes or until vegetables are tender.

4 Add shrimp, the water, bay leaf, and hot pepper sauce to skillet. Bring to boiling, stirring frequently. Cook for 1 minute more or until slightly thickened and shrimp is opaque.

5 To serve, divide rice mixture among serving bowls. Ladle shrimp mixture over rice. Sprinkle with scallions. Serve immediately. **Makes 6 servings**

Nutrition facts per serving: 508 cal., 18 g total fat (8 g sat. fat), 272 mg chol., 1,331 mg sodium, 43 g carb., 3 g dietary fiber, 4 g sugar, 41 g protein.

Bowl Bit In Cajun country, dirty rice is cooked with chicken livers or giblets, which give it a brown color. The name also refers to the confetti of green bell pepper, tomatoes, celery, and onion that flavors and colors the rice.

Lobster Newburg with Sautéed Summer Corn, Tomatoes, and Rice

START TO FINISH: 45 MINUTES

2 tablespoons butter

2 tablespoons all-purpose flour

⅓ cup dry sherry

2 cups half-and-half or light cream

2 teaspoons tomato paste

½ teaspoon salt

¼ teaspoon freshly grated nutmeg

⅛ teaspoon ground black pepper

⅛ teaspoon cayenne pepper

1 pound cooked lobster meat, cut into chunks

1 recipe Sautéed Summer Corn, Tomatoes, and Rice

¼ cup finely chopped fresh flat-leaf parsley

Paprika (optional)

1 In a large saucepan melt butter. Whisk in flour; cook and stir over medium heat for about 2 minutes or until mixture is foamy but not brown.

2 Remove from heat; slowly add sherry. Return to heat; continue stirring until mixture is smooth. Add half-and-half and tomato paste; cook and stir over medium heat until mixture comes to a boil. Reduce heat; cook for 1 minute more. Stir in salt, nutmeg, black pepper, and cayenne pepper. Gently stir in lobster; heat mixture through.

3 To serve, divide Sautéed Summer Corn, Tomatoes, and Rice among serving bowls. Spoon lobster mixture over top. Sprinkle with parsley. If desired, sprinkle with paprika. **Makes 6 servings**

Nutrition facts per serving: 526 cal., 20 g total fat (10 g sat. fat), 103 mg chol., 1,280 mg sodium, 57 g carb., 3 g dietary fiber, 5 g sugar, 25 g protein.

Sautéed Summer Corn, Tomatoes, and Rice: In a large skillet cook 2 slices chopped bacon and ½ cup chopped onion (1 medium) over medium heat for 5 minutes or until onion is tender, stirring occasionally. Add 1½ cups uncooked long grain rice, stirring to coat grains with bacon fat. Add 3¼ cups vegetable broth, corn kernels cut from 3 ears of fresh corn, and ¼ teaspoon salt. Bring to boiling; reduce heat. Simmer, covered, for 15 minutes or until broth has absorbed and rice is tender. Remove from heat. Fluff rice with fork and toss in ⅔ cup quartered grape tomatoes. Makes 6 cups.

Bowl Bit The nomenclature of this devilishly rich dish is one of its most fascinating aspects. During the 1870s, Ben Wenberg was a wealthy sea captain who shipped fruit from Cuba to New York City. During his frequent stays in the city, he dined at Delmonico's restaurant. One evening, Wenberg shared his new way of cooking lobster—in cream, butter, cognac, sherry, and cayenne pepper—with manager Charles Delmonico. It was so delicious, the restaurant added it to the menu as Lobster à la Wenberg. It was instantly in demand. A few months later, the two men had a feud. In a retaliatory huff, Delmonico removed the dish from the menu. The patrons had no problem with Wenberg, however, and continued to request the dish. Profit took precedence over revenge, and Delmonico added it back but changed the name, rearranging the letters in a clever anagram: Lobster Newberg.

Lemon-Caper Tuna and Noodles

START TO FINISH: 20 MINUTES

12 ounces dried extra-wide egg noodles

1 lemon

1 15-ounce jar light garlic Alfredo sauce, or one 10-ounce container refrigerated light Alfredo pasta sauce

1 tablespoon capers, drained

1 12-ounce can solid white albacore tuna, drained

   Ground black pepper and/or sniped fresh chives (optional)

1 Cook noodles according to package directions; drain. Cover and keep warm. Finely shred lemon zest and squeeze juice from lemon.

2 Meanwhile, in a medium saucepan combine Alfredo sauce, lemon juice, and capers; heat through.

3 Add tuna and noodles to sauce, stirring gently to combine. Return to heat just until heated through. Top with lemon zest, pepper, and chives.

Makes 4 servings

Nutrition facts per serving: 655 cal., 19 g total fat (11 g sat. fat), 154 mg chol., 1,384 mg sodium, 78 g carb., 4 g dietary fiber, 7 g sugar, 41 g protein.

Creamy Polenta with Portobello Mushroom Sauce

START TO FINISH: 40 MINUTES

2 tablespoons olive oil

2 8-ounce portobello mushrooms, stems removed, quartered, and sliced (about 7 cups)

1 large onion, finely chopped (1 cup)

6 cloves garlic, minced

¼ cup dry red wine

4 teaspoons snipped fresh oregano, or 1 teaspoon dried oregano, crushed

6 plum tomatoes, chopped

2 cups water

⅔ cup cornmeal

2 tablespoons butter

½ teaspoon salt

3 ounces Havarti or brick cheese, shredded (⅔ cup)

Fresh oregano leaves (optional)

1 In a very large skillet heat oil over medium-high heat. Add mushrooms, onion, and garlic; cook and stir for 4 to 5 minutes or until mushrooms are tender. Add wine and dried oregano (if using). Bring to boiling; reduce heat. Simmer, covered, for 5 minutes to blend flavors, stirring occasionally. Stir in tomatoes and fresh oregano (if using); heat through. Remove from heat; cover and keep warm.

2 Meanwhile, for polenta, in a medium bowl stir together 1 cup of the water and the cornmeal. In a medium saucepan bring the remaining water, the butter, and salt just to boiling. Slowly add the cornmeal mixture, stirring constantly. Reduce heat to low. Cook and stir about 10 minutes or until polenta is thick. Stir in cheese.

3 To serve, divide polenta among shallow pasta or soup bowls. Top with mushroom mixture. If desired, garnish fresh oregano leaves. **Makes 4 servings**

Nutrition facts per serving: 377 cal., 21 g total fat (2 g sat. fat), 26 mg chol., 345 mg sodium, 33 g carb., 8 g dietary fiber, 5 g sugar, 12 g protein.

White Bean Chili with Toasted Cumin

PREP: 30 MINUTES   **COOK:** 1 HOUR

- 3 tablespoons vegetable oil
- 2 cups chopped onions (2 large)
- 6 cloves garlic, minced
- 4 14.5-ounce cans diced tomatoes, undrained
- 2 12-ounce cans beer or nonalcoholic beer
- 2 canned chipotle chile peppers in adobo sauce, chopped
- 2 tablespoons cumin seeds, toasted*
- 2 teaspoons sugar
- 1 teaspoon salt
- 4 19-ounce cans baby or regular white kidney (cannellini) or white navy beans, rinsed and drained
- 3 cups coarsely chopped, seeded, and peeled golden nugget, butternut, and/or acorn squash (about 12 ounces)
- 1 8-ounce carton sour cream
- ¼ cup lime juice
- 2 tablespoons snipped fresh chives

1 In a 6- to 8-quart Dutch oven heat oil over medium heat. Add onions and garlic; cook and stir until onion is tender. Stir in tomatoes, beer, chile peppers, cumin seeds, sugar, and salt. Stir in beans. Bring to boiling; reduce heat. Stir in squash. Simmer, covered, for 1 hour.

2 Meanwhile, in a small bowl combine sour cream, lime juice, and chives. Top each serving with sour cream mixture. **Makes 8 servings**

Nutrition facts per serving: 365 cal., 15 g total fat (5 g sat. fat), 13 mg chol., 995 mg sodium, 52 g carb., 13 g dietary fiber, 17 g protein.

*Note: *To toast cumin seeds, place the seeds in a dry skillet over low heat. Cook about 8 minutes, stirring often.*

Polenta with Eggs and Zucchini

START TO FINISH: 40 MINUTES

½ cup dried tomatoes, cut up

2¼ cups milk

1 14-ounce can reduced-sodium chicken broth

1 cup yellow cornmeal (polenta)

⅓ cup grated Parmesan cheese

1 tablespoon olive oil

1 small onion, thinly sliced

2 small zucchini and/or yellow summer squash, thinly sliced lengthwise

1 small yellow or green sweet pepper, cut into strips

Salt and ground black pepper

1 small lemon

8 eggs

Fresh flat-leaf parsley and/or shaved Parmesan cheese (optional)

1 In a small bowl cover dried tomatoes with boiling water. In a large saucepan combine milk and broth; bring just to boiling over high heat. Gradually whisk in cornmeal. Reduce heat to medium-low. Cook, stirring frequently, for 12 to 15 minutes, until thick and creamy. Stir in grated cheese. Reduce heat to low; cover and keep warm.

2 Meanwhile, drain tomatoes. In a large skillet heat oil over medium heat. Add tomatoes, onion, zucchini, and sweet pepper; cook 3 to 5 minutes or until tender. Season with salt and pepper. Remove from heat; cover and keep warm.

3 In another large deep skillet add water to half-full. Squeeze half of lemon into skillet. Cut remaining half into wedges. Bring lemon water to a simmer. Break eggs one at a time into a small cup and slide into water. Cook eggs 4 at a time in simmering lemon water for 4 to 5 minutes or until whites are firm and yolks are firm but still a little soft. Remove with a slotted spoon; drain on paper towel–lined plate.

4 To serve, ladle polenta into bowls and top with zucchini mixture and 2 poached eggs. Sprinkle with fresh parsley and/or shaved cheese. Serve with lemon wedges. **Makes 4 servings**

Nutrition facts per serving: 465 cal., 21 g total fat (8 g sat. fat), 445 mg chol., 953 mg sodium, 44 g carb., 6 g dietary fiber, 14 g sugar, 29 g protein.

Kitchen Tip If you have a mandoline slicer, use it to make almost paper-thin slices of zucchini or yellow squash. You can also use the large-blade side of a box grater.

Make-It-Mine American Bowl

PREP: 35 MINUTES   COOK: 2 TO 2 HOURS 10 MINUTES

Meat, page 186

½ cup all-purpose flour

2 tablespoons canola oil

Onion Mixture, page 186

Broth and Seasoning, page 186

Vegetable Mixture, page 187

Salt and ground black pepper

Toppers, page 187

1 In a medium bowl toss Meat with all-purpose flour. Shake off and discard any excess flour. In a Dutch oven or large heavy pot heat oil over medium-high heat. Add Meat to hot oil without crowding; cook about 5 minutes or until brown on all sides, turning frequently. Cook in batches (if necessary, add additional oil). Return all meat to pan.

2 Add Onion Mixture; cook and stir for 4 minutes. Add Broth and Seasoning. Bring mixture to boiling; reduce heat. Simmer, covered, about 1½ hours (20 minutes for Moroccan Chicken Stew) or until meat is tender, stirring occasionally. Add some water if stew gets too thick.

3 Add Vegetables Mixture. Bring mixture to boiling; reduce heat. Simmer, covered, for 30 to 40 minutes or until vegetables are tender, stirring occasionally. Season to taste with salt and black pepper.

4 Meanwhile, in a small bowl stir together Toppers ingredients. To serve, ladle hot stew into bowls and add Toppers mixture. **Makes 6 servings**

MEAT

Hearty Beef Stew with Mustard Cream

2 pounds boneless beef chuck, trimmed of fat and cut into 1-inch pieces

Moroccan Chicken Stew

2 pounds skinless, boneless chicken thighs

Mediterranean Lamb Stew

2 pounds boneless lamb shoulder, trimmed of fat and cut into 1-inch pieces, or lamb stew meat

Pork, Sweet Potato, and Black Bean Stew

2 pounds boneless pork shoulder, trimmed of fat and cut into 1-inch pieces

ONION MIXTURE

Hearty Beef Stew with Mustard Cream

½ cup chopped onion (1 medium)

¾ cup chopped sweet red pepper (1 medium)

3 cloves garlic, thinly sliced

2 teaspoons coriander seeds, crushed

2 teaspoons ground turmeric

2 teaspoons ground cumin

¼ teaspoon ground allspice

Moroccan Chicken Stew

½ cup chopped onion (1 medium)

4 cloves garlic, minced

Mediterranean Lamb Stew

½ cup chopped onion (1 medium)

4 cloves garlic, minced

Pork, Sweet Potato, and Black Bean Stew

1 medium red onion, cut into thin wedges

¾ cup chopped yellow sweet pepper (1 medium)

4 cloves garlic, minced

2 teaspoons ground cumin

BROTH + SEASONING

Hearty Beef Stew with Mustard Cream

4 cups reduced-sodium chicken broth

2 teaspoons grated fresh ginger

1 to 2 fresh serrano chile peppers, stemmed and sliced*

1 3-inch stick cinnamon (remove before serving)

Moroccan Chicken Stew

3 cups reduced-sodium chicken broth

2 cups dry white wine

2 teaspoons snipped fresh rosemary

2 bay leaves (remove before serving)

Mediterranean Lamb Stew

3 cups reduced-sodium chicken broth

2 cups dry white wine

2 teaspoons snipped fresh rosemary

2 bay leaves (remove before serving)

Pork, Sweet Potato, and Black Bean Stew

4 cups reduced-sodium chicken broth

2 14.5-ounce cans stewed tomatoes, undrained

3 fresh jalapeno chile peppers, seeds and membranes removed and sliced*

VEGETABLE MIXTURE

Hearty Beef Stew with Mustard Cream

- 1½ pounds red or white new potatoes, halved
- 5 carrots, peeled and cut into 1-inch pieces
- 8 ounces white mushrooms, halved
- 1 cup thawed frozen pearl onions
- ¼ cup chopped fresh flat-leaf parsley

Moroccan Chicken Stew

- 1 pound butternut squash, peeled, seeded, and cut into 1½-inch pieces
- 4 carrots, sliced ½ inch thick
- 1 15-ounce can chickpeas, rinsed and drained
- ½ cup orange juice
- ½ cup pitted green olives
- ⅓ cup dried apricots, cut into strips
- 1 tablespoon lemon juice

Mediterranean Lamb Stew

- 1 14.5-ounce can diced tomatoes, undrained
- 1½ cups dried lentils (soak for 10 minutes and drain)
- 2 medium bulbs fennel, trimmed, cored, and cut into wedges
- 1 small leek, thinly sliced (white and light green portions only)
- 8 large fresh basil leaves, torn

Pork, Sweet Potato, and Black Bean Stew

- 5 medium tomatillos, coarsely chopped
- 2 medium sweet potatoes, peeled and cut into 2-inch pieces
- 1 15-ounce can black beans, rinsed and drained
- 1 tablespoon lime juice

TOPPERS

Hearty Beef Stew with Mustard Cream

- ¾ cup whipping cream, whipped to soft peaks
- 1 tablespoon coarse-grain mustard
- 2 teaspoons prepared horseradish

Moroccan Chicken Stew

- ½ cup plain Greek yogurt
- 3 tablespoons snipped fresh mint
- 2 teaspoons honey
- 1 teaspoon finely shredded orange zest

Mediterranean Lamb Stew

- ⅓ cup crumbled feta cheese
- ¼ cup quartered, pitted kalamata olives
- 3 tablespoons snipped fresh flat-leaf parsley

Pork, Sweet Potato, and Black Bean Stew

- ⅓ cup snipped fresh cilantro
- 1 tablespoon finely shredded lime zest
- 3 cloves garlic, minced

*Note: *Because chile peppers contain volatile oils that can burn your skin and eyes, avoid direct contact with them as much as possible. When working with chile peppers, wear plastic or rubber gloves. If your bare hands do touch the chile peppers, wash your hands well with soap and water.*

The Salad
bowl

Asian-Style Beef Salad

PREP: 35 MINUTES   BROIL: 12 MINUTES   MARINATE: 2 TO 8 HOURS   OVEN: BROIL

12 ounces boneless beef sirloin steak, cut 1-inch thick

1 fresh jalapeño chile pepper, seeded and finely chopped*

½ teaspoon finely shredded lime zest

3 tablespoons lime juice

2 tablespoons reduced-sodium soy sauce

1 tablespoon snipped fresh cilantro

2 teaspoons toasted sesame oil

1 teaspoon sugar

2 cloves garlic, minced

6 cups coarsely shredded napa cabbage and/or bok choy

½ cup red sweet pepper strips or fresh peapods, tips and strings removed

¼ cup sliced scallions (2)

1 Preheat broiler. Trim fat from steak. Place steak on the unheated rack of a broiler pan. Broil 3 to 4 inches from the heat for 12 to 15 minutes or until desired doneness (160°F for medium doneness). Let stand for 5 minutes. Cut steak across the grain into thin bite-size strips.

2 Meanwhile, in a medium bowl stir together chile pepper, lime zest, lime juice, soy sauce, cilantro, oil, sugar, and garlic. Stir in beef. Cover and marinate in the refrigerator for 2 to 8 hours.

3 To serve, in a large bowl toss together napa cabbage and/or bok choy, sweet pepper or pea pods, and scallions. Stir beef mixture; arrange in center of cabbage mixture. **Makes 4 servings**

Nutrition facts per serving: 166 cal., 6 g total fat (1 g sat. fat), 40 mg chol., 346 mg sodium, 9 g carb., 2 g dietary fiber, 4 g sugar, 21 g protein.

*Note: *Because chile peppers contain volatile oils that can burn your skin and eyes, avoid direct contact with them as much as possible. When working with chile peppers, wear plastic gloves. If your bare hands touch the chile peppers, wash your hands well with soap and water.*

Beefy Pasta Salad

START TO FINISH: 30 MINUTES

1 cup dried penne pasta (about 3½ ounces)

2 ears of corn, husks and silks removed

Nonstick cooking spray

12 ounces boneless beef sirloin steak, trimmed of fat, cut into thin bite-size strips, or 2 cups shredded cooked beef pot roast (10 ounces)

1 cup cherry tomatoes, halved

¼ cup shredded fresh basil

2 tablespoons finely shredded Parmesan cheese

3 tablespoons white wine vinegar

1 tablespoon olive oil

1 clove garlic, minced

¼ teaspoon salt

⅛ teaspoon ground black pepper

¼ cup finely shredded Parmesan cheese

1 In a 4- to 6-quart Dutch oven cook pasta according to package directions, adding corn for the last 3 minutes of cooking time. Using tongs, transfer corn to a large cutting board. Drain pasta. Rinse in cold water; drain again. Set aside. Cool corn until easy to handle.

2 Meanwhile, coat an unheated large nonstick skillet with cooking spray. Preheat skillet over medium-high heat. Add beef strips; cook for 4 to 6 minutes or until slightly pink in the center, stirring occasionally. (If using shredded beef, cook until heated through.) Remove from heat; cool slightly.

3 On a cutting board place an ear of corn pointed end down. While holding corn firmly at stem end to keep in place, use a sharp knife to cut corn from cobs, leaving corn in planks; rotate cob as needed to cut corn from all sides. Repeat with the remaining ear of corn. In a large bowl combine pasta, beef, tomatoes, basil, and the 2 tablespoons cheese.

4 In a screw-top jar combine vinegar, oil, garlic, salt, and pepper. Cover and shake well. Pour over pasta mixture; toss gently to coat. Gently fold in corn planks or place corn planks on top of individual servings. Serve immediately. Garnish with ¼ cup cheese. **Makes 4 servings**

Nutrition facts per serving: 313 cal., 10 g total fat (3 g sat. fat), 41 mg chol., 341 mg sodium, 28 g carb., 4 g dietary fiber, 3 g sugar, 28 g protein.

Kitchen Tip If you have leftover beef pot roast, simply shred the meat and use 2 cups of it in the salad.

Mediterranean Beef Salad with Lemon Vinaigrette

PREP: 20 MINUTES   **BROIL:** 15 MINUTES   **OVEN:** BROIL

- 1 **pound boneless beef top sirloin steak, cut 1 inch thick**
- ¼ **teaspoon salt**
- ⅛ **teaspoon ground black pepper**
- 4 **cups torn romaine lettuce**
- ½ **of a small red onion, thinly sliced and separated into rings (½ cup)**
- 1 **cup halved cherry or grape tomatoes**
- ½ **cup crumbled feta cheese (2 ounces)**
- 1 **recipe Lemon Vinaigrette**

1 Trim fat from steak. Sprinkle steak with salt and pepper. Place steak on the unheated rack of a broiler pan. Broil 3 to 4 inches from the heat until desired doneness, turning once halfway through broiling time. Allow 15 to 17 minutes for medium-rare doneness (145°F) or 20 to 22 minutes for medium doneness (160°F). Thinly slice steak.

2 Divide lettuce among serving bowls. Top with sliced meat, red onion, tomatoes, and cheese. Drizzle with Lemon Vinaigrette. **Makes 4 servings**

Nutrition facts per serving: 323 cal., 21 g total fat (5 g sat. fat), 81 mg chol., 402 mg sodium, 7 g carb., 2 g dietary fiber, 27 g protein.

Lemon Vinaigrette: In a screw-top jar combine ¼ cup olive oil; ½ teaspoon finely shredded lemon zest; 3 tablespoons lemon juice; 1 tablespoon snipped fresh oregano or 1 teaspoon dried oregano, crushed; and 2 cloves garlic, minced. Cover and shake well. Season to taste with salt and black pepper. Makes about ½ cup.

Taco Salad Bowls

PREP: 35 MINUTES   BAKE: 10 MINUTES   OVEN: 350°F

4 6- to 8-inch whole wheat or plain flour tortillas

Nonstick cooking spray

12 ounces lean ground beef or ground turkey

½ cup chopped onion (1 medium)

1 clove garlic, minced

1 8-ounce can tomato sauce

1 tablespoon cider vinegar

½ teaspoon ground cumin

¼ teaspoon crushed red pepper

4 cups shredded lettuce

¼ cup shredded reduced-fat cheddar cheese (1 ounce)

¼ cup chopped green or red sweet pepper (optional)

12 cherry tomatoes, quartered

1 Preheat oven to 350°F. For tortilla bowls, wrap tortillas in foil. Heat in oven for 10 minutes. Coat four 10-ounce custard cups with cooking spray. Carefully press 1 tortilla into each cup. Bake for 10 to 15 minutes or until golden and crisp. Cool tortillas bowls in custard cups on wire rack; remove bowls from custard cups. Set aside.

2 Meanwhile, in a large skillet cook ground beef, onion, and garlic until meat is brown and onion is tender. Drain off fat.

3 Stir tomato sauce, vinegar, cumin, and crushed red pepper into mixture in skillet. Bring to boiling; reduce heat. Simmer, uncovered, for 10 minutes.

4 Place tortilla bowls in serving bowls. Spoon meat mixture into bowls. Sprinkle with lettuce, cheese, sweet pepper (if using), and tomatoes. **Makes 4 servings**

Nutrition facts per serving: 297 cal., 13 g total fat (4 g sat. fat), 59 mg chol., 575 mg sodium, 23 g carb., 3 g dietary fiber, 22 g protein.

Kitchen Tip Making your own tortilla bowls saves a lot on fat and calories over the store-bought variety. You can make the bowls a day ahead: After they've baked, cool completely, then store in an airtight container at room temperature. Right before serving, crisp them in a 300°F oven for 5 minutes.

Pork and Noodle Salad

PREP: 25 MINUTES   **BAKE:** 30 MINUTES   **CHILL:** UP TO 24 HOURS   **OVEN:** 425°F

1 recipe Ginger-Soy Dressing

1 ¾- to 1-pound pork tenderloin
   Salt and ground black pepper

1 3.75-ounce package bean threads
   or cellophane noodles

2 cups shredded napa cabbage

2 medium carrots, shredded

1 cup thinly sliced radishes

2 cups torn bok choy or baby bok choy

½ cup fresh cilantro leaves

1 recipe Wonton Crisps

1 Prepare Ginger-Soy Dressing; set aside.

2 Preheat oven to 425°F. Line 15x10x1-inch pan with foil. Trim fat from pork; place in prepared pan. Sprinkle with salt and pepper. Roast for 25 minutes, or until thermometer registers 155°F, brushing with 1 tablespoon of the dressing during the last 5 minutes of cooking. Cover with foil and let stand for 15 minutes. Slice thinly.

3 Meanwhile, prepare noodles according to package directions. Rinse with cold water to cool; drain well. Using clean kitchen scissors, snip noodles into short lengths. In a large bowl toss noodles and cabbage.

4 In a 3-quart rectangular dish layer noodle mixture, carrots, pork, and radishes. Drizzle with half of the Ginger-Soy dressing. Top with bok choy and cilantro. Chill, covered, until ready to serve or up to 24 hours. Serve with Wonton Crisps; pass remaining dressing. **Makes 6 servings**

Nutrition facts per serving: 351 cal., 17 g total fat (2 g sat. fat), 38 mg chol., 529 mg sodium, 35 g carb., 2 g dietary fiber, 8 g sugar, 15 g protein.

Ginger-Soy Dressing: In screw-top jar combine ⅓ cup vegetable oil, 3 tablespoons lime juice, 3 tablespoons rice vinegar, 1 tablespoon packed brown sugar, 1 tablespoon grated fresh ginger, 1 tablespoon honey, 1 tablespoon soy sauce, 1 teaspoon toasted sesame oil, ¼ teaspoon salt, and ¼ teaspoon crushed red pepper. Cover and shake well. Refrigerate for up to 3 days.

Wonton Crisps: Preheat oven to 425°F. Line baking sheet with foil. Lightly coat with nonstick cooking spray. Place 12 wonton wrappers on baking sheet. Brush tops of wrappers with 1 tablespoon sesame or peanut oil. Bake for 5 to 6 minutes or until golden (wontons will continue to brown after baking). When cool, break into pieces.

Buffalo Chicken Salad

PREP: 20 MINUTES   **MARINATE:** 30 MINUTES   **BROIL:** 14 MINUTES   **OVEN:** BROIL

½ cup mayonnaise

¼ cup bottled barbecue sauce

½ cup crumbled blue cheese
(about 3 ounces)

2 tablespoons milk

1 teaspoon bottled hot pepper sauce

1¼ pounds boneless, skinless chicken
breast halves

½ teaspoon bottled hot pepper sauce

4 cups torn iceberg lettuce
(about 1 head)

3 cups torn romaine lettuce
(about 1 head)

2 stalks celery, cut into 1- to 2-inch-
long matchsticks

1 large carrot, peeled and cut into
2-inch-long matchsticks

1 tablespoon crumbled blue cheese

1 For dressing, in a small bowl combine mayonnaise, barbecue sauce, ½ cup cheese, milk, and 1 teaspoon hot pepper sauce.

2 Place chicken in a resealable plastic bag set in a shallow dish. Add ⅓ cup of the dressing and ½ teaspoon hot pepper sauce. Seal bag, turning to coat chicken. Marinate in the refrigerator for 30 minutes.

3 Preheat broiler. Drain chicken, discarding the marinade. Place chicken on the unheated rack of a broiler pan. Broil 4 to 5 inches from heat for 8 minutes. Turn chicken and broil 6 minutes more or until chicken is no longer pink (170°F).

4 Meanwhile, in a large bowl toss together lettuces, celery, and carrot. Add remaining dressing to greens in bowl. Cut chicken into thin slices. Place over salad. Sprinkle with 1 tablespoon cheese. **Makes 6 servings**

Nutrition facts per serving: 318 cal., 22 g total fat (6 g sat. fat), 76 mg chol., 488 mg sodium, 6 g carb., 2 g dietary fiber, 24 g protein.

Bowl Bit Created in 1964 at the Anchor Bar and Restaurant in Buffalo, New York, Buffalo wings have since spread their spicy goodness all over the world—more recently in the form of pizza, potato chips, popcorn chicken, and, of course, salads. One October night, college student Dominic Bellissimo was working late at his parents' bar. A group of hungry friends came in and he asked his mother, Teressa, to fix a snack. Teressa had an excess of chicken wings—a part that usually went into the soup pot. She deep-fried the wings, tossed them with a cayenne hot sauce, and served them with blue cheese dressing and celery sticks. A classic was born.

Chicken and Quinoa Salad with Roasted Chiles

PREP: 45 MINUTES   COOK: 25 MINUTES   ROAST: 20 MINUTES   STAND: 45 MINUTES   OVEN: 425°F

8   ounces fresh Anaheim chile peppers, poblano chile peppers, banana chile peppers, and/or red sweet peppers*

1   cup quinoa**

1   cup water

3   tablespoons lime juice

2   tablespoons olive oil

2   cloves garlic, minced

¼   teaspoon salt

¼   teaspoon ground black pepper

1½ cups shredded cooked chicken or cooked pork

⅓   cup sliced almonds or pine nuts, toasted

½   cup coarsely chopped fresh cilantro

½   cup chopped scallions (4)

   Bibb or Boston lettuce leaves

1 Preheat oven to 425°F. Cut chile peppers in half lengthwise. Remove stems, seeds, and membranes. Place pepper halves, cut side down, on a foil-lined baking sheet. Roast for 20 to 25 minutes or until skins are blistered and dark. Carefully fold foil up and around pepper halves to enclose; let stand about 15 minutes. Using a sharp knife, loosen edges of the skins; gently and slowly pull off the skin in strips. Cut peppers into bite-size strips; set aside.

2 Place uncooked quinoa in a fine-mesh sieve; thoroughly rinse with cold water and drain. In a medium saucepan combine quinoa and the water. Bring to boiling; reduce heat. Simmer, covered, for 25 minutes. Remove from heat. Uncover; let stand for 30 minutes.

3 For dressing, in a small screw-top jar combine lime juice, olive oil, garlic, salt, and black pepper. Cover and shake well.

4 In a large bowl combine roasted chile pepper strips, cooked quinoa, dressing, chicken, almonds, cilantro, and scallion; toss to combine. Line serving bowls with lettuce. Top with chicken salad. **Makes 4 or 5 servings**

Nutrition facts per serving: 454 cal., 22 g total fat (3 g sat. fat), 50 mg chol., 220 mg sodium, 43 g carb., 5 g dietary fiber, 26 g protein.

*Note: *Because hot chile peppers contain volatile oils that can burn your skin and eyes, avoid direct contact with chiles as much as possible. When working with chile peppers, wear plastic or rubber gloves. If your bare hands do touch the peppers, wash your hands well with soap and water.*

**Note: *If desired, substitute 2 cups couscous for the quinoa. Cook the couscous according to package directions.*

Chicken Waldorf Salad

START TO FINISH: 20 MINUTES **CHILL:** UP TO 24 HOURS

12 ounces cooked skinless, boneless chicken breast, shredded or cubed (2 cups)

2 cups coarsely chopped red and/or green apples (2 medium)

¼ cup thinly sliced celery

⅓ cup dried tart cherries

⅓ cup coarsely chopped pecans or peanuts

⅓ cup mayonnaise

⅓ cup sour cream

1 to 1½ teaspoons dried rosemary, crushed

1 tablespoon lemon juice

1 tablespoon honey

Lettuce leaves

1 In a medium bowl toss together chicken, apples, celery, cherries, and nuts. For dressing, in a small bowl combine mayonnaise, sour cream, rosemary, lemon juice, and honey. Add to chicken mixture; toss to coat.

2 Cover and chill for up to 24 hours. Serve on lettuce leaves. **Makes 4 servings**

Nutrition facts per serving: 468 cal., 28 g total fat (6 g sat. fat), 88 mg chol., 192 mg sodium, 30 g carb., 4 g dietary fiber, 28 g protein.

Bowl Bit Waldorf Salad—a sweet and crunchy combination of apples, grapes, celery, and walnuts tossed in a mayonnaise dressing— has the singular distinction of being mentioned in a Cole Porter song— "You're the Top" from the 1934 musical *Anything Goes*. Dreamed up sometime between 1893 and 1896 by Oscar Tschirky, the maître d'hôtel at the Waldorf Hotel in New York City, the salad was already the stuff of culinary legend when Porter wrote: "You're the top!/You're a Waldorf salad/You're the top!/You're a Berlin ballad."

Ginger-Chicken Pasta Salad

PREP: 35 MINUTES   **CHILL:** 4 TO 24 HOURS

- 1 **pound dried rotini or small bow tie pasta**
- 3 **cups snow peas, tips and strings removed**
- ⅓ **cup salad oil**
- ⅓ **cup rice vinegar**
- ¼ **cup sugar**
- ¼ **cup soy sauce**
- 1 **tablespoon grated fresh ginger**
- 1 **teaspoon crushed red pepper**
- 1¼ **pounds cooked chicken, cut into bite-size strips (4 cups)**
- 3 **cups yellow and/or red sweet pepper strips (3 medium)**
- 1½ **cups thinly sliced radishes**
- 1 **cup bias-sliced scallions (8)**
- ⅓ **cup snipped fresh cilantro or parsley**
- 1 **cup chopped peanuts**

1 Cook pasta according to package directions; drain. Rinse pasta with cold water; drain again.

2 Meanwhile, cook snow peas, covered, in boiling water for 30 seconds; drain. Rinse peas with cold water; drain again. Cover and chill until serving time.

3 For dressing, in a screw-top jar combine oil, vinegar, sugar, soy sauce, ginger, and crushed red pepper. Cover and shake well.

4 In a very large bowl toss together cooked pasta, chicken, pepper strips, radishes, scallions, and cilantro. Add dressing; toss gently to coat. Cover and chill for 4 to 24 hours.

5 Just before serving, add pea pods and toss mixture together. Sprinkle with peanuts. **Makes 10 to 12 servings**

Nutrition facts per serving: 484 cal., 20 g total fat (3 g sat. fat), 50 mg chol., 492 mg sodium, 48 g carb., 5 g dietary fiber, 7 g sugar, 28 g protein.

Crispy Chopped Chicken Salad

PREP: 45 MINUTES   **BAKE:** 8 MINUTES   **COOK:** 8 MINUTES   **OVEN:** 400°F

6 thin slices prosciutto (about 4 ounces)

½ cup extra-virgin olive oil

4 skinless, boneless chicken breast halves

Salt and ground black pepper

Paprika

2 lemons

2 tablespoons finely chopped shallot (1)

2 small carrots, peeled and thinly sliced

2½ cups chopped zucchini (2 medium)

¾ cup chopped red sweet pepper (1 medium)

¾ cup chopped yellow sweet pepper (1 medium)

½ of a small red onion, chopped

5 ounces blue cheese, crumbled

Romaine lettuce leaves

1 Preheat oven to 400°F. Place prosciutto in single layer on large baking sheet. Bake for 8 to 10 minutes or until crisp. Set aside.

2 In a large nonstick skillet heat 1 tablespoon of the oil over medium heat. Sprinkle chicken with salt, black pepper, and paprika. Add chicken to skillet; cook for 8 to 10 minutes or until chicken is no longer pink (170°F), turning once. Cool chicken slightly; slice.

3 For dressing, finely shred zest from 1 lemon; squeeze lemons to make ⅓ cup juice. In small bowl whisk together the remaining oil, shredded zest, lemon juice, and shallot. Season with salt and pepper.

4 In a large bowl combine chicken, carrots, zucchini, sweet peppers, and onion. Add dressing; toss to coat. Add cheese.

5 Line salad bowls with romaine. Spoon chicken mixture into lettuce-lined bowls. Top with prosciutto. **Makes 6 servings**

Nutrition facts per serving: 425 cal., 28 g total fat (8 g sat. fat), 86 mg chol., 965 mg sodium, 10 g carb., 2 g dietary fiber, 4 g sugar, 34 g protein.

Spicy Thai Noodle Salad

START TO FINISH: 30 MINUTES

⅔ cup reduced-sodium chicken broth

¼ cup creamy peanut butter

3 tablespoons seasoned or plain rice vinegar

1 tablespoon reduced-sodium soy sauce

1 teaspoon toasted sesame oil

⅛ teaspoon cayenne pepper

8 ounces dried Chinese egg noodles, or one 9-ounce package dried angel hair pasta

6 to 7 ounces deli-roasted chicken breast, skinned and shredded (1½ cups)

1½ cups packaged shredded carrot

1 small cucumber, seeded and cut into thin bite-size strips

¼ cup slivered fresh basil

2 tablespoons coarsely chopped peanuts (optional)

1 For dressing, in a small saucepan combine broth and peanut butter; cook and stir over low heat until peanut butter is melted. Remove from heat. Whisk in vinegar, soy sauce, oil, and cayenne pepper. Set aside.

2 Prepare noodles or pasta according to package directions, except omit oil or salt; drain.

3 In a large bowl toss together noodles, chicken, carrot, cucumber, and basil. Drizzle with dressing; toss to coat. If desired, sprinkle with peanuts. **Makes 4 servings**

Nutrition facts per serving: 366 cal., 11 g total fat (2 g sat. fat), 36 mg chol., 554 mg sodium, 44 g carb., 3 g dietary fiber, 5 g sugar, 25 g protein.

Greek Chicken Salad

PREP: 30 MINUTES   **MARINATE:** 4 TO 24 HOURS   **GRILL:** 12 MINUTES

4 **skinless, boneless chicken breast halves**

1 **tablespoon lemon juice**

1 **tablespoon olive oil**

1 **tablespoon snipped fresh oregano, or 1 teaspoon dried oregano, crushed**

¼ **teaspoon ground black pepper**

2 **cloves garlic, minced**

3 **medium cucumbers, seeded and cut into ½-inch pieces**

2 **medium tomatoes, cut into ½-inch pieces**

½ **cup chopped red onion (1 medium)**

   Mixed salad greens (optional)

⅓ **cup bottled creamy cucumber salad dressing**

½ **cup crumbled feta cheese (2 ounces)**

¼ **cup chopped pitted kalamata olives or other black olives**

1 Place chicken in a resealable plastic bag set in a shallow dish. For marinade, in a small bowl combine lemon juice, oil, oregano, pepper, and garlic. Pour over chicken. Seal bag; turn to coat chicken. Marinate in the refrigerator for 4 to 24 hours, turning bag occasionally.

2 In a medium bowl toss together cucumbers, tomatoes, and red onion. Set aside.

3 Drain chicken, discarding marinade. For a charcoal grill, place chicken on the rack of an uncovered grill directly over medium coals. Grill for 12 to 15 minutes or until tender and no longer pink (170°F), turning once. (For a gas grill, preheat grill. Reduce heat to medium. Place chicken on grill rack over heat. Cover; grill as directed.)

4 Transfer chicken to a cutting board; cut into bite-size pieces. Toss chicken with cucumber mixture. If desired, serve on greens. Drizzle chicken-cucumber mixture with salad dressing. Sprinkle with feta cheese and olives. **Makes 4 servings**

Nutrition facts per serving: 391 cal., 20 g total fat (5 g sat. fat), 95 mg chol., 483 mg sodium, 16 g carb., 3 g dietary fiber, 37 g protein.

Goi Ga (Vietnamese Chicken Salad)

PREP: 10 MINUTES   COOK: 5 MINUTES   STAND: 20 MINUTES   CHILL: UP TO 24 HOURS

2 medium skinless, boneless chicken breast halves

½ of a red onion, halved and sliced (½ cup)

¼ cup lime juice

3 tablespoons water

3 tablespoons rice vinegar

2 tablespoons canola oil

1 tablespoon sugar

1 tablespoon fish sauce

2 teaspoons grated fresh ginger

1 to 2 small red chile peppers, halved, seeded, and thinly sliced*

2 cloves garlic, minced

2 shallots, thinly sliced

5 cups finely shredded napa cabbage

1 cup coarsely shredded carrots (2 medium)

½ cup chopped fresh cilantro leaves

⅓ cup chopped fresh basil and/or mint leaves

⅓ cup unsalted dry-roasted peanuts, coarsely chopped

1 In a large skillet combine chicken, red onion, and enough cold water to cover. Bring to boiling over medium-high heat; reduce heat. Simmer, covered, for 5 minutes. Remove from heat; let stand for 20 minutes. (After standing, chicken should be no longer pink and an instant-read thermometer should register 170°F.) Using a slotted spoon, transfer chicken and onions to a medium bowl. Cover and chill for 30 minutes. Discard cooking liquid.

2 Meanwhile, for dressing, in a small bowl whisk together lime juice, the 3 tablespoons water, vinegar, oil, sugar, fish sauce, ginger, chile peppers, and garlic. Whisk until sugar is dissolved; stir in shallots. Cover and chill until ready to serve.

3 In a very large serving bowl combine cabbage, carrots, cilantro, and basil. Cover and chill until ready to serve or up to 24 hours.

4 When ready to serve, shred chicken into bite-size pieces. Add chicken and onions to cabbage mixture. Pour dressing mixture over; toss to coat. Top with peanuts. **Makes 4 servings**

Nutrition facts per serving: 299 cal., 15 g total fat (2 g sat. fat), 49 mg chol., 438 mg sodium, 18 g carb., 3 g dietary fiber, 9 g sugar, 25 g protein.

*Note: *Because hot chile peppers contain volatile oils that can burn your skin and eyes, avoid contact with chiles as much as possible. When working with chile peppers, wear plastic or rubber gloves. If your bare hands do touch the chile peppers, wash your hands well with soap and water.*

Kitchen Tip The traditional method for preparing the chicken for this ethereally light and crunchy salad is to poach it—but if you have leftover roasted or grilled chicken, that works fine, too.

Thai Chicken Noodle Salad

START TO FINISH: 20 MINUTES **CHILL:** UP TO 2 HOURS

1 2½-pound deli-roasted chicken

4 cups water

2 3-ounce packages ramen noodles (any flavor)

¾ cup creamy peanut butter

¾ cup unsweetened light coconut milk

⅓ cup lime juice

¼ cup chopped fresh cilantro

1 tablespoon sugar

¾ teaspoon salt

¼ to ½ teaspoon cayenne pepper

⅔ cup sliced scallions (6)

1 small cucumber, peeled, seeded, halved lengthwise, and cut into ¼-inch slices

Coarsely chopped peanuts (optional)

1 Discard skin from chicken. Remove meat from bones; cut into strips. In a medium saucepan bring the water to boiling. Break each package of noodles into 4 pieces (reserve seasoning packets for another use). Add noodles to boiling water. Remove from heat; let stand, covered, 5 minutes. Drain noodles. Rinse noodles with cold water; drain. Set aside.

2 Meanwhile, in a large bowl whisk together peanut butter, coconut milk, lime juice, cilantro, sugar, salt, and cayenne pepper until smooth. Add chicken, noodles, scallions, and cucumber; toss to coat.

3 Serve immediately or cover and chill for up to 2 hours. If desired, garnish with peanuts. **Makes 6 servings**

Nutrition facts per serving: 670 cal., 35 g total fat (10 g sat. fat), 142 mg chol., 663 mg sodium, 30 g carb., 3 g dietary fiber, 6 g sugar, 59 g protein.

Warm Chicken Salad with Oranges and Almonds

START TO FINISH: 20 MINUTES

2 medium oranges

6 cups torn romaine lettuce

1 medium red sweet pepper, cut into bite-size strips

½ of a small red onion, halved and thinly sliced

⅓ cup slivered or sliced almonds, toasted

1 pound skinless, boneless chicken breast strips for stir-frying, or 1 pound skinless, boneless chicken breast halves, cut into thin bite-size strips

   Salt and ground black pepper

2 tablespoons olive oil

⅓ cup orange juice

1 tablespoon red wine vinegar

1 teaspoon Dijon mustard

1 Peel oranges. Cut into ¼-inch slices; quarter each orange slice. In a large bowl toss together orange slices, romaine, sweet pepper, onion, and almonds.

2 Season chicken with salt and black pepper. In a large skillet cook chicken in 1 tablespoon hot oil for 4 to 5 minutes or until no longer pink, stirring occasionally. Remove skillet from heat. Toss chicken with mixture in salad bowl. Divide salad among bowls.

3 Stir orange juice and vinegar into the hot skillet, scraping up any brown bits in the skillet. Whisk in the remaining oil and the mustard. Drizzle warm dressing on top of salads. Season to taste with additional black pepper. **Makes 4 servings**

Nutrition facts per serving: 310 cal., 16 g total fat (2 g sat. fat), 59 mg chol., 161 mg sodium, 17 g carb., 5 g dietary fiber, 26 g protein.

Mediterranean Tabbouleh Salad with Chicken

PREP: 30 MINUTES   **CHILL:** 4 TO 24 HOURS   **STAND:** 30 MINUTES

1½ cups water

½ cup bulgur

1 cup chopped tomatoes (2 medium)

1 cup finely chopped seeded cucumber

1 cup finely chopped fresh flat-leaf parsley

⅓ cup thinly sliced scallions (3)

¼ cup snipped fresh mint, or 1 tablespoon dried mint, crushed

⅓ to ½ cup lemon juice

¼ cup olive oil

½ teaspoon salt

½ teaspoon ground black pepper

12 large leaves romaine and/or butterhead (Bibb or Boston) lettuce

18 ounces cooked skinless, boneless chicken breast halves,* sliced

1 In a large bowl combine the water and bulgur. Let stand for 30 minutes. Drain bulgur through a fine-mesh sieve, using a large spoon to press out excess water. Return bulgur to bowl. Stir in tomatoes, cucumber, parsley, scallions, and mint.

2 For dressing, in a screw-top jar combine lemon juice, oil, salt, and pepper. Cover and shake well. Pour dressing over the bulgur mixture. Toss lightly to coat. Cover and chill for 4 to 24 hours, stirring occasionally. Bring to room temperature before serving.

3 Serve romaine with bulgur mixture and cooked chicken. **Makes 6 servings**

Nutrition facts per serving: 294 cal., 13 g total fat (2 g sat. fat), 72 mg chol., 276 mg sodium, 16 g carb., 5 g dietary fiber, 3 g sugar, 30 g protein.

*Note: *To broil chicken breast halves, preheat broiler. Lightly sprinkle chicken with salt and black pepper. Place chicken on the unheated rack of a broiler pan. Broil chicken 4 to 5 inches from heat for 12 to 15 minutes or until chicken is no longer pink (170°F), turning once halfway through broiling.*

Bowl Bit Nearly anywhere you go in the Arab world, there is some version of this light and nutty-tasting salad of bulgur, tomatoes, mint, and scallions tossed with a garlicky olive oil–lemon dressing. The proportion of grains to greens varies from place to place—as does the exact name—but the main elements stay essentially the same. In Arabic, *tabbule* means "little spicy."

Warm Polenta Zucchini Salad with Chicken

- 2 **medium zucchini**
  Salt and ground black pepper
- 3½ **tablespoons extra-virgin olive oil**
- ½ **16-ounce package prepared polenta, cut into ¾-inch cubes**
- 5 **cups baby mixed greens or baby arugula (2½ ounces)**
- 2 **boneless, skinless chicken breasts, cooked and shredded (1¾ cups total)**
- 2 **tablespoons red wine vinegar**
- 1 **tablespoon chopped fresh oregano**
- ½ **teaspoon sugar**
- ½ **teaspoon kosher salt**
- ½ **cup crumbled blue cheese (3 ounces)**

1 Cut zucchini in half lengthwise. Cut zucchini halves on the bias into ¼-inch slices. Sprinkle with salt and pepper. Heat 1½ teaspoons oil in a large nonstick skillet over high heat. Add zucchini; cook and stir about 3 minutes or until golden. Transfer zucchini to a large bowl. Reduce heat to medium. Add polenta to skillet; cook and stir about 4 minutes or until heated through. Add to bowl with zucchini. Add greens and chicken to bowl; toss.

2 Whisk together the remaining oil, the vinegar, oregano, sugar, and kosher salt. Add half of the vinaigrette to the zucchini mixture; toss to coat. Arrange salad on a platter and sprinkle with blue cheese. Serve with remaining vinaigrette. **Makes 4 servings**

Nutrition facts per serving: 350 cal., 21 g total fat (7 g sat. fat), 69 mg chol., 583 mg sodium, 10 g carb., 2 g dietary fiber, 27 g protein.

Chopped Turkey Club Salad with Creamy Horseradish Dressing

PREP: 35 MINUTES   **BAKE:** 5 MINUTES   **OVEN:** 425°F

3 slices firm-textured white bread, cut into ½-inch cubes

1 tablespoon butter, melted

3 cups chopped iceberg lettuce

3 cups chopped red leaf lettuce

8 ounces sliced peppered deli turkey, chopped

5 slices peppered bacon, crisp-cooked, drained, and crumbled

4 hard-cooked eggs, coarsely chopped

1 cup cubed provolone cheese (4 ounces)

1 cup grape or cherry tomatoes, quartered

½ cup chopped red onion (1 medium)

½ cup chopped celery (1 stalk)

1 recipe Creamy Horseradish Dressing

10 lemon wedges

1 Preheat oven to 425°F. In a large bowl toss together bread cubes and melted butter. Spread cubes in a shallow baking pan. Bake for 5 minutes or until toasted.

2 In a large bowl combine lettuces, turkey, bacon, eggs, cheese, tomatoes, onion, and celery. Toss to combine. Add Creamy Horseradish Dressing and toss to coat. Sprinkle each serving with croutons and serve with a lemon wedge. **Makes 10 servings**

Creamy Horseradish Dressing: In a small bowl combine ½ cup mayonnaise, 2 tablespoons cider vinegar, 2 to 4 teaspoons prepared horseradish, 2 teaspoons sugar, 2 teaspoons cracked black pepper, ½ teaspoon finely shredded lemon zest, 1 teaspoon lemon juice, 1 minced clove garlic, ¼ teaspoon salt, and ¼ teaspoon cayenne pepper.

Nutrition facts per serving: 244 cal., 17 g total fat (5 g sat. fat), 115 mg chol., 673 mg sodium, 11 g carb., 2 g dietary fiber, 3 g sugar, 13 g protein.

Warm Salmon and Arugula Pasta Salad

START TO FINISH: 40 MINUTES   **OVEN:** BROIL

1   1½-pound salmon fillet with skin

2   teaspoons grated lemon zest

1   teaspoon ground coriander

1½ teaspoons kosher salt

2   teaspoons extra-virgin olive oil

1   pound dried linguine fini

2   cups grape tomatoes, halved

1   small shallot, peeled and thinly sliced lengthwise

1   4-ounce package soft mild plain goat cheese, crumbled

5   ounces baby arugula

3   tablespoons olive oil

    Crumbled goat cheese (optional)

    Ground black pepper (optional)

1 Preheat broiler. Line a large baking sheet with foil. Rinse salmon; pat dry with paper towels. Place salmon skin side down on baking sheet. In a small bowl combine half of lemon zest, the coriander, and ½ teaspoon kosher salt. Brush top of salmon with 2 teaspoons oil; rub with lemon mixture. Let stand at room temperature for 10 minutes.

2 Meanwhile, cook pasta according to package directions; drain.

3 Broil salmon 4 to 5 inches from heat for 8 to 10 minutes or until fish begins to flake when tested with a fork. Cool salmon slightly. Remove and discard skin.

4 Flake salmon into a large bowl. Add the remaining lemon zest, the remaining kosher salt, the pasta, the tomatoes, shallot, cheese, arugula, and 3 tablespoons oil to bowl; toss gently to combine. If desired, garnish with additional cheese and season with pepper. Serve immediately. **Makes 4 to 6 servings**

Nutrition facts per serving: 730 cal., 29 g total fat (8.5 g sat. fat), 90 mg chol., 668 mg sodium, 73 g carb., 4 g dietary fiber, 42 g protein.

Kitchen Tip *Linguine fini* is a thinner version of linguine. If you can't find it, use regular or thin spaghetti.

Lemon Shrimp and Bread Salad

PREP: 30 MINUTES   **MARINATE:** 1 HOUR   **GRILL:** 16 MINUTES   **STAND:** 20 MINUTES

- 1 **pound fresh or frozen large shrimp**
- 3 **tablespoons olive oil**
- 1 **teaspoon lemon-pepper seasoning**
- 2 **large pita bread rounds**
- 2 **yellow sweet peppers, quartered lengthwise and seeded**
- 1 **cup chopped tomatoes (2 medium)**
- ½ **cup chopped English cucumber or cucumber**
- ¼ **cup sliced radishes**
- ¼ **cup sliced scallions (2)**
- ¼ **cup bottled red wine vinaigrette**
  Salt and ground black pepper

1 Thaw shrimp, if frozen. Peel and devein shrimp. Rinse shrimp; pat dry with paper towels. Place shrimp in a medium bowl. For marinade, stir together 2 tablespoons of the oil and the lemon-pepper seasoning. Toss shrimp with marinade. Cover and marinate in the refrigerator for 1 hour, stirring occasionally. Thread shrimp on four long metal skewers, leaving a ¼-inch space between shrimp. Lightly brush pita bread and sweet pepper quarters with the remaining oil.

2 For a charcoal grill, grill sweet pepper quarters, cut sides up, on the rack of an uncovered grill directly over medium-hot coals about 10 minutes or until pepper skins are blistered. Remove sweet peppers from grill. Wrap peppers in foil and let stand for 20 minutes. Meanwhile, grill shrimp for 6 to 8 minutes or until shrimp turn opaque, turning once halfway through grilling. Grill pita bread for 2 to 4 minutes or until lightly toasted, turning once halfway through grilling. (For a gas grill, preheat grill. Reduce heat to medium-hot. Place sweet peppers, cut sides up, and shrimp and bread on grill rack over heat. Cover and grill as directed.)

3 Peel and coarsely chop sweet peppers. Cut pita into 1-inch pieces. Remove shrimp from skewers. In a large bowl combine grilled sweet peppers, bread, and shrimp. Stir in tomatoes, cucumber, radishes, and scallions. Drizzle with vinaigrette. Toss gently to coat. Season to taste with salt and black pepper. Serve immediately. **Makes 4 to 6 servings**

Nutrition facts per serving: 376 cal., 17 g total fat (2 g sat. fat), 172 mg chol., 802 mg sodium, 28 g carb., 2 g dietary fiber, 5 g sugar, 27 g protein.

Pasta Salad Niçoise

PREP: 30 MINUTES   **COOK:** 22 MINUTES

8 ounces fresh green beans

1 pound dried shell-shaped pasta

1 small cucumber, seeded and chopped

1 small red onion, halved and thinly sliced crosswise

2 cups cherry tomatoes, halved

2 6-ounce cans chunk white tuna (water pack), drained and broken into chunks

½ cup kalamata olives, pitted and halved

2 teaspoons Dijon mustard

⅓ cup lemon juice

3 tablespoons red wine vinegar

1½ teaspoons sugar

½ teaspoon salt

¼ teaspoon dried oregano, crushed

Pinch ground black pepper

⅔ cup olive oil

1 Remove ends and strings from beans. Cut into 1½-inch pieces. In a large saucepan cook beans, covered, in a small amount of boiling water for 3 to 4 minutes or until crisp-tender; drain. Immediately plunge beans in ice water; let sit for 3 minutes or until cool. Drain well; set aside.

2 In same saucepan cook pasta according to package directions; drain. Rinse pasta with cold water; drain again.

3 In a large bowl toss together green beans, pasta, cucumber, red onion, tomatoes, tuna, and olives.

4 For dressing, whisk together mustard, lemon juice, vinegar, sugar, salt, oregano, and pepper. While whisking, add oil in a thin stream; continue to whisk the dressing until smooth and the oil is thoroughly incorporated. Pour dressing over salad; gently toss to coat. **Makes 12 servings**

Nutrition facts per serving: 325 cal., 15 g total fat (2 g sat. fat), 10 mg chol., 303 mg sodium, 36 g carb., 3 g dietary fiber, 12 g protein.

Shrimp Caesar Salad

PREP: 20 MINUTES   **CHILL:** 30 MINUTES

1 pound peeled and deveined cooked shrimp

1 16-ounce can artichoke hearts, drained, or one 9-ounce package frozen artichoke hearts, thawed, drained, and quartered

¾ cup bottled Caesar salad dressing

2 tablespoons lemon juice

½ teaspoon salt

¼ teaspoon ground black pepper

1 clove garlic, halved

12 cups torn or cut-up romaine lettuce leaves

1 cup seasoned croutons

¼ cup grated Parmesan cheese

8 flat or rolled canned anchovies (optional)

1 In a medium bowl toss together shrimp, artichoke hearts, ¼ cup of the dressing, the lemon juice, salt, and pepper. Cover and chill for 30 minutes, stirring occasionally.

2 Rub inside of a large bowl with cut sides of garlic; discard clove. Add lettuce, the remaining dressing, and croutons to the bowl; toss. Top with shrimp mixture and sprinkle with cheese. If desired, garnish with anchovies. **Makes 4 servings**

Nutrition facts per serving: 398 cal., 21 g total fat (5 g sat. fat), 261 mg chol., 1,386 mg sodium, 17 g carb., 5 g dietary fiber, 36 g protein.

Spicy Shrimp Tabbouleh

PREP: 30 MINUTES   **CHILL:** 4 TO 24 HOURS

1⅓ cups water

⅔ cup bulgur

½ cup bottled fat-free ranch salad dressing

½ teaspoon finely shredded lime zest

2 tablespoons lime juice

¼ teaspoon crushed red pepper

1 cup peapods, halved crosswise

½ cup chopped radishes or daikon

½ cup snipped fresh cilantro

¼ cup bias-sliced scallions (2)

8 ounces peeled and deveined cooked shrimp, halved lengthwise

1 In a small saucepan combine the water and bulgur. Bring to boiling; reduce heat. Simmer, covered, about 15 minutes or until most of the water is absorbed and bulgur is tender.

2 Meanwhile, for dressing, in a small bowl combine ranch dressing, lime zest, lime juice, and crushed red pepper. Cover and chill.

3 Stir pea pods into bulgur; transfer to a large bowl. Add radishes, cilantro, scallions, and dressing; toss to coat. Cover and chill for 4 to 24 hours. Just before serving, stir in shrimp. **Makes 4 servings**

Nutrition facts per serving: 201 cal., 1 g total fat (0 g sat. fat), 111 mg chol., 495 mg sodium, 32 g carb., 6 g dietary fiber, 16 g protein.

Shrimp, Corn, and Goat Cheese Pasta Salad

START TO FINISH: 1 HOUR

- 1 **pound large shrimp, peeled and deveined**
- 3 **tablespoons extra-virgin olive oil**
- 3 **cups fresh whole kernel corn**
- 1 **pound grape tomatoes, halved**
- 4 **ounces orzo**
- 2 **cups torn butter lettuce leaves**
- 2 **ounces soft mild goat cheese, crumbled**
- ½ **cup fresh basil leaves**
- 3 **tablespoons lime juice**
- **Salt and ground black pepper**
- **Lime wedges (optional)**

1 Rinse shrimp; pat dry with paper towels. In a large skillet cook shrimp in 1½ tablespoons hot oil over medium-high heat about 2 minutes or until shrimp are opaque. Transfer shrimp to a medium bowl. Wipe skillet clean.

2 Add the remaining oil to clean skillet; cook corn and tomatoes in hot oil about 3 minutes or until tender. Toss corn mixture with shrimp in bowl. Cool mixture to room temperature for 20 to 25 minutes, stirring occasionally.

3 Meanwhile, in a large pot cook orzo according to package directions; drain. Add orzo to shrimp mixture in bowl. Stir in lettuce, cheese, basil, and lime juice. Season to taste with salt and pepper. If desired, serve with lime wedges. **Makes 6 servings**

Nutrition facts per serving: 310 cal., 12 g total fat (3 g sat. fat), 98 mg chol., 145 mg sodium, 34 g carb., 4 g dietary fiber, 20 g protein.

Peachy Lobster Pasta Salad

START TO FINISH: 30 MINUTES

6 ounces dried medium shell macaroni (2 cups)

½ cup snipped mixed fresh herbs such as basil, dill, and thyme

¼ cup olive oil

1 teaspoon finely shredded lime zest

3 tablespoons lime juice

3 tablespoons orange juice

2 cloves garlic, minced

1 tablespoon honey

¼ teaspoon salt

¼ teaspoon ground black pepper

3 medium peaches, peeled and sliced

2 cups cut-up cooked lobster or crabmeat (cartilage removed) or flake-style imitation lobster (12 ounces cooked)

1 cup watercress

1 Cook pasta according to package directions; drain. Rinse pasta with cold water; drain.

2 Meanwhile, in a large bowl combine herbs, oil, lime zest, lime juice, orange juice, garlic, honey, salt, and pepper. Add peach slices; toss gently to combine. Add pasta, lobster, and watercress. Toss gently to combine. Season to taste with additional salt and pepper. **Makes 4 to 6 servings**

Nutrition facts per serving: 422 cal., 15 g total fat (2 g sat. fat), 61 mg chol., 509 mg sodium, 49 g carb., 3 g dietary fiber, 14 g sugar, 24 g protein.

Kitchen Tip Watercress has a lovely, peppery flavor that complements the sweetness of the peaches and lobster. If you can't find fresh watercress, arugula makes a fine substitute.

Fiesta Quinoa Salad

PREP: 20 MINUTES   **CHILL:** 2 TO 24 HOURS

1   cup quinoa

1   15-ounce can black beans, rinsed and drained

1   cup packaged julienned carrots

¾   cup chopped yellow or red sweet pepper (1 medium)

⅓   cup chopped red onion

1   fresh jalapeño chile pepper, seeded and finely chopped*

¼   cup snipped fresh cilantro

¼   cup olive oil

1   teaspoon finely shredded lime zest

3   tablespoons lime juice

1   teaspoon salt

1   teaspoon ground cumin

1 Place quinoa in a fine-mesh strainer. Rinse under cold running water; drain. In a medium saucepan bring 2½ cups water to boiling. Add quinoa. Return to boiling; reduce heat. Simmer, covered, for 10 minutes. Drain in the fine-mesh strainer. Rinse with cold water; drain again. Place in a large bowl.

2 Add beans, carrots, sweet pepper, red onion, chile pepper, and cilantro to bowl. For dressing, in a small bowl stir together oil, lime zest, lime juice, salt, and cumin. Add to vegetable mixture. Toss to coat. Cover and chill for 2 to 24 hours. **Makes 6 servings**

Nutrition facts per serving: 191 cal., 8 g total fat (1 g sat. fat), 0 mg chol., 440 mg sodium, 26 g carb., 5 g dietary fiber, 7 g protein.

*Note: *Because chile peppers contain volatile oils that can burn your skin and eyes, avoid direct contact with them as much as possible. When working with chile peppers, wear plastic or rubber gloves. If your bare hands do touch the peppers, wash your hands and nails well with soap and warm water.*

Kitchen Tip Quinoa is something of a miracle grain. A staple food of the Aztecs, it is a complete protein, with all eight of the essential amino acids. Additionally, it has the highest protein content of any grain—as well as one of the lowest levels of carbohydrates of any grain. Although it is lighter than rice, it can be used in place of rice in most recipes.

Greek Garbanzo Salad

PREP: 35 MINUTES   CHILL: 4 TO 24 HOURS

1 15- to 16-ounce can garbanzo beans (chickpeas), rinsed and drained

2 cups seeded and chopped cucumber (1 medium)

1 cup coarsely chopped tomatoes (2 medium)

1 cup coarsely chopped green sweet pepper (1 large)

½ cup thinly sliced red onion

2 tablespoons olive oil

2 tablespoons red wine vinegar

1 tablespoon finely snipped fresh mint

1 tablespoon lemon juice

2 cloves garlic, minced

½ cup crumbled reduced-fat feta cheese (2 ounces)

Salt and ground black pepper

2 cups torn mixed salad greens or romaine lettuce

1 In a large bowl combine garbanzo beans, cucumber, tomatoes, sweet pepper, and red onion.

2 For dressing, in a small bowl whisk together oil, vinegar, mint, lemon juice, and garlic. Pour dressing over garbanzo bean mixture; toss to coat. Cover and chill for 4 to 24 hours.

3 To serve, stir feta cheese into salad. Season to taste with salt and black pepper. Serve over mixed greens. **Makes 4 servings**

Nutrition facts per serving: 200 cal., 10 g total fat (3 g sat. fat), 5 mg chol., 694 mg sodium, 25 g carb., 7 g dietary fiber, 6 g sugar, 11 g protein.

Mediterranean Quinoa-Edamame Salad

PREP: 20 MINUTES   COOK: 15 MINUTES   CHILL: UP TO 24 HOURS

½ cup quinoa, rinsed and drained

1 cup water

1 cup ready-to-eat fresh or thawed frozen shelled sweet soybeans (edamame)

2 medium roma tomatoes, seeded and chopped

¾ cup shredded spinach

¼ cup finely chopped red onion

2 tablespoons olive oil

2 tablespoons lemon juice

2 tablespoons snipped fresh basil

¼ teaspoon salt

¼ teaspoon ground black pepper

2 tablespoons reduced-fat feta cheese

1 In a medium saucepan combine quinoa and the water. Bring to boiling; reduce heat. Simmer, covered, about 15 minutes or until quinoa is tender and liquid is absorbed, adding edamame during the last 4 minutes of cooking.

2 In a large bowl combine quinoa mixture, tomatoes, spinach, and red onion.

3 For dressing, in a small bowl whisk together oil and lemon juice. Stir in basil, salt, and pepper. Add dressing to quinoa mixture; toss to coat. Sprinkle with cheese. Serve immediately or cover and chill for up to 24 hours. **Makes 4 servings**

Nutrition facts per serving: 225 cal., 11 g total fat (2 g sat. fat), 1 mg chol., 220 mg sodium, 22 g carb., 5 g dietary fiber, 4 g sugar, 10 g protein.

Tabbouleh with Edamame and Feta

PREP: 25 MINUTES   **COOK:** 15 MINUTES

2½ cups water

1¼ cups bulgur

¼ cup lemon juice

3 tablespoons purchased pesto

2 cups ready-to-eat fresh or thawed frozen sweet soybeans (edamame)

2 cups cherry tomatoes, cut up

⅓ cup crumbled reduced-fat feta cheese

⅓ cup thinly sliced scallions (3)

2 tablespoons snipped fresh parsley

¼ teaspoon ground black pepper

Fresh parsley sprigs (optional)

1 In a medium saucepan combine the water and bulgur. Bring to boiling; reduce heat. Simmer, covered, about 15 minutes or until most of the liquid is absorbed. Transfer bulgur to a large bowl.

2 In a small bowl whisk together lemon juice and pesto; stir into cooked bulgur. Add soybeans, tomatoes, cheese, scallions, parsley, and pepper. Toss gently to combine. If desired, garnish with parsley sprigs. **Makes 6 servings**

Nutrition facts per serving: 313 cal., 12 g total fat (1 g sat. fat), 3 mg chol., 187 mg sodium, 37 g carb., 10 g dietary fiber, 18 g protein.

Panzanella

PREP: 35 MINUTES   STAND: 35 MINUTES

1   **fennel bulb**

3   **tablespoons red wine vinegar**

1   **tablespoon balsamic vinegar**

4   **cloves garlic, minced**

½   **teaspoon kosher salt**

¼   **teaspoon ground black pepper**

⅔   **cup extra-virgin olive oil**

5   **cups dry bread cubes***

1   **pint grape tomatoes, halved**

1   **medium red onion, very thinly sliced**

1   **seedless cucumber, thinly sliced**

½   **cup snipped fresh basil**

3   **ounces Parmesan cheese, shaved**

1 Cut off and discard fennel stalks. Remove any wilted outer layers; cut bulb into thin slices.

2 In a small bowl combine vinegars, garlic, salt, and pepper. While whisking vigorously, add oil gradually until combined.

3 In a large bowl toss bread cubes with 2 tablespoons of the vinaigrette. Let stand for 5 minutes. Add tomatoes, red onion, cucumber, and basil; toss well.

4 Add remaining vinaigrette and cheese; toss well. Let stand at room temperature for 30 to 45 minutes before serving. **Makes 6 servings**

Nutrition facts per serving: 391 cal., 29 g total fat (6 g sat. fat), 10 mg chol., 613 mg sodium, 25 g carb., 3 g dietary fiber, 5 g sugar, 9 g protein.

*Note: *Cut day-old rustic Italian white bread into 1-inch cubes. Place on a baking sheet. Bake in a 300°F oven for 20 minutes or until bread is dry and crisp. (Or let bread cubes stand at room temperature overnight to dry.)*

Bowl Bit Thrifty Italian cooks who wasted nothing invented this chunky bread salad. Instead of tossing day-old or dry bread, they made it into bread soup (*pappa al pomodoro*) or salad (*panzanella*). Day-old bread is cut into chunks and tossed with onions, tomatoes, olive oil, vinegar, herbs, and cheese.

Udon Noodles with Tofu

START TO FINISH: 25 MINUTES

8 ounces dried udon (Japanese) noodles or whole wheat linguine

2 6- to 8-ounce packages smoked teriyaki-flavored or plain firm tofu, cut into ½-inch pieces

1½ cups chopped cucumber

1 large carrot, cut into thin bite-size pieces

½ cup sliced scallions (4)

1 recipe Ginger-Soy Vinaigrette

1 Cook pasta according to package directions; drain. Cool pasta slightly.

2 Meanwhile, in a large bowl toss together tofu, cucumber, carrot, and scallions. Add pasta; toss gently to mix.

3 Drizzle Ginger-Soy Vinaigrette over pasta mixture. Toss salad gently to coat. **Makes 6 servings**

Ginger-Soy Vinaigrette: In a small bowl whisk together 2 tablespoons rice vinegar or cider vinegar, 1 tablespoon toasted sesame oil, 2 teaspoons reduced-sodium soy sauce, 4 minced cloves garlic, 1 teaspoon grated fresh ginger, and ¼ teaspoon crushed red pepper. Makes ¼ cup.

Nutrition facts per serving: 231 cal., 4 g total fat (0 g sat. fat), 0 mg chol., 571 mg sodium, 39 g carb., 3 g dietary fiber, 7 g protein.

Make-It-Mine Salad Bowl

PREP: 35 MINUTES

Noodles and/or Greens, below

Savory Additions, page 240

Salad Dressing, page 240

Toppers, page 241

1 Place Noodles and/or Greens in a large serving bowl. Top with Savory Additions.

2 In a medium bowl whisk together Salad Dressing ingredients. Pour over greens or noodle mixture in serving bowl; toss to coat.

3 Top salad with Toppers and toss again. **Makes 4 servings**

NOODLES AND/OR GREENS

Asian

- 3 cups cooked, drained, and cooled Asian-style noodles (rice, egg, or soba), cut up
- 2 cups finely shredded savoy cabbage

Classic Chopped

- 5 cups chopped iceberg or romaine lettuce

Autumn Harvest

- 4 cups mixed torn greens or baby greens
- 2 cups watercress, tough stems removed

Southwest

- 4 cups chopped romaine lettuce
- 1 cup shredded red cabbage

SAVORY ADDITIONS

Asian

1½ cups shredded cooked chicken

 1 small red sweet pepper, cut into bite-size strips

 ½ cup shredded carrot (1 medium)

 ½ cup thinly sliced daikon

 ½ cup sliced snow peas

 ½ of an 8-ounce can sliced water chestnuts, drained

 ¼ cup fresh cilantro leaves

Classic Chopped

 1 cup chopped tomatoes (2 medium)

 1 cup chopped cucumber (1 small)

 3 ounces cheddar cheese, diced

 ½ cup chopped celery (1 stalk)

 ⅓ cup chopped roasted red sweet pepper (1 small)

 ⅓ cup finely chopped red onion (1 small)

 ¼ cup sliced radishes

Autumn Harvest

 2 medium beets, cooked, peeled, cooled, and sliced
    (or use canned sliced beets)

1½ cups cooked and cooled lentils

 1 ripe pear, peeled, cored, and sliced

 3 ounces crumbled feta cheese

 ½ cup chopped cooked ham (optional)

 ¼ cup dried apricots cut into strips

Southwest

1½ cups chopped smoked turkey

 1 cup cooked black beans (or used canned black
    beans, rinsed and drained)

 1 avocado, halved, pitted, peeled, and chopped

 1 mango, pitted, peeled, and chopped

 ¾ cup cooked fresh or thawed frozen whole
    kernel corn

 ½ of a small jicama, peeled and cut into
    bite-size strips

SALAD DRESSING

Asian

- ⅓ cup canola oil
- ¼ cup rice vinegar
- 2 tablespoons finely chopped shallot (1 medium)
- 2 tablespoons reduced-sodium soy sauce
- 1 tablespoon lemon juice
- 1 tablespoon toasted sesame seeds
- 1 teaspoon grated fresh ginger
- ⅛ to ¼ teaspoon crushed red pepper

Classic Chopped

- ¼ cup crumbled blue cheese
- 3 tablespoons mayonnaise
- 3 tablespoons sour cream
- 1 tablespoon Dijon-style mustard
- 1 tablespoon canola oil
- 1 tablespoon white wine vinegar
- ½ teaspoon cracked black pepper

Autumn Harvest

- ⅓ cup canola oil
- 3 tablespoons apricot nectar
- 3 tablespoons cider vinegar
- 1 tablespoon maple syrup
- 2 teaspoons Dijon-style mustard
- ½ teaspoon salt
- ¼ teaspoon cracked black pepper

Southwest

- ⅓ cup canola oil
- 3 tablespoons lime juice
- 2 teaspoons honey
- 1 chipotle chile pepper in adobo sauce, finely chopped
- ½ teaspoon salt
- ½ teaspoon ground cumin

TOPPERS

Asian

- 1 11-ounce can mandarin orange sections, drained
- ¼ cup sliced scallions (2)
- ¼ cup dried wasabi peas

Classic Chopped

- 3 slices bacon, crisp-cooked, drained, and crumbled
- 3 hard-cooked eggs, peeled and sliced
  Crumbled blue cheese

Autumn Harvest

- ¼ cup toasted walnuts, chopped
- 3 tablespoons toasted sunflower nuts
  Crumbled feta cheese

Southwest

- ½ cup coarsely crushed tortilla chips
- 3 tablespoons toasted pepitas

Index

Note: Page references in *italics* indicate photographs.

Metric Information

The charts on this page provide a guide for converting measurements from the U.S. customary system, which is used throughout this book, to the metric system.

PRODUCT DIFFERENCES

Most of the ingredients called for in the recipes in this book are available in most countries. However, some are known by different names. Here are some common American ingredients and their possible counterparts:

- Sugar (white) is granulated, fine granulated, or castor sugar.
- Powdered sugar is icing sugar.
- All-purpose flour is enriched, bleached, or unbleached white household flour. When self-rising flour is used in place of all-purpose flour in a recipe that calls for leavening, omit the leavening agent (baking soda or baking powder) and salt.
- Light-colored corn syrup is golden syrup.
- Cornstarch is cornflour.
- Baking soda is bicarbonate of soda.
- Vanilla or vanilla extract is vanilla essence.
- Green, red, or yellow sweet peppers are capsicums or bell peppers.
- Golden raisins are sultanas.

VOLUME AND WEIGHT

The United States traditionally uses cup measures for liquid and solid ingredients. The chart, top right, shows the approximate imperial and metric equivalents. If you are accustomed to weighing solid ingredients, the following approximate equivalents will be helpful.

- 1 cup butter, castor sugar, or rice = 8 ounces = ½ pound = 250 grams
- 1 cup flour = 4 ounces = ¼ pound = 125 grams
- 1 cup icing sugar = 5 ounces = 150 grams

Canadian and U.S. volume for a cup measure is 8 fluid ounces (237 ml), but the standard metric equivalent is 250 ml.

1 British imperial cup is 10 fluid ounces.

In Australia, 1 tablespoon equals 20 ml, and there are 4 teaspoons in the Australian tablespoon.

Spoon measures are used for smaller amounts of ingredients. Although the size of the tablespoon varies slightly in different countries, for practical purposes and for recipes in this book, a straight substitution is all that's necessary. Measurements made using cups or spoons always should be level unless stated otherwise.

COMMON WEIGHT RANGE REPLACEMENTS

Imperial / U.S.	Metric
½ ounce	15 g
1 ounce	25 g or 30 g
4 ounces (¼ pound)	115 g or 125 g
8 ounces (½ pound)	225 g or 250 g
16 ounces (1 pound)	450 g or 500 g
1¼ pounds	625 g
1½ pounds	750 g
2 pounds or 2¼ pounds	1,000 g or 1 Kg

OVEN TEMPERATURE EQUIVALENTS

Fahrenheit Setting	Celsius Setting*	Gas Setting
300°F	150°C	Gas Mark 2 (very low)
325°F	160°C	Gas Mark 3 (low)
350°F	180°C	Gas Mark 4 (moderate)
375°F	190°C	Gas Mark 5 (moderate)
400°F	200°C	Gas Mark 6 (hot)
425°F	220°C	Gas Mark 7 (hot)
450°F	230°C	Gas Mark 8 (very hot)
475°F	240°C	Gas Mark 9 (very hot)
500°F	260°C	Gas Mark 10 (extremely hot)
Broil	Broil	Grill

*Electric and gas ovens may be calibrated using celsius. However, for an electric oven, increase celsius setting 10 to 20 degrees when cooking above 160°C. For convection or forced air ovens (gas or electric) lower the temperature setting 25°F/10°C when cooking at all heat levels.

BAKING PAN SIZES

Imperial / U.S.	Metric
9×1½-inch round cake pan	22- or 23×4-cm (1.5 L)
9×1½-inch pie plate	22- or 23×4-cm (1 L)
8×8×2-inch square cake pan	20×5-cm (2 L)
9×9×2-inch square cake pan	22- or 23×4.5-cm (2.5 L)
11×7×1½-inch baking pan	28×17×4-cm (2 L)
2-quart rectangular baking pan	30×19×4.5-cm (3 L)
13×9×2-inch baking pan	34×22×4.5-cm (3.5 L)
15×10×1-inch jelly roll pan	40×25×2-cm
9×5×3-inch loaf pan	23×13×8-cm (2 L)
2-quart casserole	2 L

U.S. / STANDARD METRIC EQUIVALENTS

⅛ teaspoon = 0.5 ml	⅓ cup = 3 fluid ounces = 75 ml
¼ teaspoon = 1 ml	½ cup = 4 fluid ounces = 125 ml
½ teaspoon = 2 ml	⅔ cup = 5 fluid ounces = 150 ml
1 teaspoon = 5 ml	¾ cup = 6 fluid ounces = 175 ml
1 tablespoon = 15 ml	1 cup = 8 fluid ounces = 250 ml
2 tablespoons = 25 ml	2 cups = 1 pint = 500 ml
¼ cup = 2 fluid ounces = 50 ml	1 quart = 1 litre